D1463528

Big Game Wisdom

Hunting Wisdom Library ™

MINNETONKA, MINNESOTA

BIG GAME WISDOM
Edited by Tom Carpenter

Printed in 2009.

Tom Carpenter
Creative Director

Jen Weaverling
Managing Editor

Heather Koshiol
Senior Book Development Coordinator

Shari Gross
Production Coordinator

Zachary Marell
Book Design and Production

9 10 / 13 12 11 10 09
ISBN 978-1-58159-103-3
© 2000 North American Hunting Club

North American Hunting Club
12301 Whitewater Drive
Minnetonka, Minnesota 55343
www.huntingclub.com

Table of Contents

INTRODUCTION

From cornfield whitetails to mountain sheep and everywhere in between, Big Game Wisdom *takes you where the game is and shows you how to hunt successfully.*

There's only one problem, if you can call it that, with this book *Big Game Wisdom*: It will make you want to hunt every one of the North American game animals within its pages, as if there isn't already enough hunting to pack into an autumn.

That's what happened to me anyway. As the words poured in and the pictures came together and each chapter took shape I'd think either: "Oh yes, I do love to hunt that game, and I'm going to do more of it," or "Man, I *have* to do that before I die."

My bet is that *Big Game Wisdom* will keep you busy reading and learning ... and busier than ever hunting as well. You'll find quarry in here that you hunt every year, perhaps whitetails or bears. You'll find game you want to hunt more often or maybe for the first time: possibly elk, mulies, moose, pronghorns or even sheep. And there are some animals you probably thought you'd never hunt but now you'll get the itch—caribou, goats, Coues' deer, blacktails, maybe even a musk ox. We've even added a chapter on the big game bird—our wild turkey—that hooks so many big game hunters.

These words and pictures capture the wisdom you need to know to hunt each of these great North American big game animals effectively and with more success. You'll go hunting with a true expert on each species, because no one person could bring you this depth and detail.

Opposite page: Buck mule deer testing the breeze.

Glassing the big country.

• Come to whitetail country—North, South, East, West and Everywhere In Between—with Gary Clancy, one of the most well-traveled and hard-working whitetail hunters we know.

• Head to the Southwestern desert and hunt Coues' deer with Patrick Meitin, a true addict of these tiny but challenging whitetails, and a very successful guide on trophy bucks.

• Chase elk with Jim Zumbo, one of North America's top outdoor writers but, more impor-

tant, a real hunter who knows elk and what it takes to get one.

• Hunt mule deer with the best—hunter, writer and rancher Jim Van Norman of Wyoming, who simplifies the process of finding and hunting big buck mule deer. They still exist!

• Sneak around blacktail country with Bob Robb, another *hunter* who also knows how to write, and knows what it takes to ferret out good bucks.

• Take the fair-chase challenge and tag along on a pronghorn hunt with me. I may not be the world's best pronghorn hunter, but I guarantee no one loves them, or antelope country, more.

• Feel your heart beat a little harder when Jim Shockey talks bears and bear hunting. He knows how to make you feel like you're right there—and helps you learn something in the process.

• Stalk our biggest deer, a bull moose, with Judd Cooney, a veteran of innumerable moose haunts and hunts, both in the West and the Far North.

• Discover caribou with Wayne van Zwoll, and let his words help you realize that the hunt is about being there in caribou country more than anything else.

• Set out after all four of our magnificent wild sheep with bowhunter Chuck Adams, and let him present years' worth of insights that both rifle hunters and archers can use. He even admits to shooting his first sheep with a rifle!

• Climb to alpine peaks and cliffs, again with Bob Robb, who makes his personal goat hunting equation even more difficult by carrying archery gear.

• Go on a true arctic adventure—for musk ox—with Jim Shockey, someone brave enough to tackle polar elements *and* a game animal that can be quite ornery.

Blacktail buck.

You may never hunt a musk ox, but Big Game Wisdom *will take you to musk ox country and show you how it's done.*

• Set up in the turkey woods with Glenn Sapir—a passionate and highly successful turkey hunter who can teach you the essentials of getting on birds, and getting them to come to you, both spring and fall.

Each writer has his own style, and each one takes you down a different trail, at a different pace and in a different way. But that's what makes *Big Game Wisdom* so fun to read, and such a valuable reference tool for your hunting book collection. The bottom line is always the same: Each story will make you an even better hunter, more knowledge-able about the game as well as the strategies, techniques and equipment for hunting it.

Take the wisdom of these words and pictures along when you hit the woods, fields, riverbottoms, hills, mountains, prairie, tundra, desert or anywhere else the game takes you: You will hunt smart, hunt better and increase your chances for success. It's time to take another leg on the lifelong trail to *Big Game Wisdom.*

Tom

Tom Carpenter
Editor, North American Hunting Club Books

Let Big Game Wisdom *broaden your hunting horizons: with down-to-earth advice that will help you better hunt the game you love; and with ideas and guidance for branching out to hunt wonderful and exciting North American big game you haven't yet pursued.*

Chapter 1

WHITETAILS: EAST, WEST, EVERYWHERE

By Gary Clancy

Whitetails are everywhere these days—from Western mountains (shown here) to Carolina swamps. But that doesn't make deer hunting one bit easier. Author Gary Clancy presents no-nonsense, straightforward hunting how-to that even veteran whitetail chasers can take to the woods, fields, swamps and mountains.

East, West or anywhere in between, these are heady times if you hunt whitetails. Forget about the "good old days" your father, grandfather and uncles all talk about; the good old days in the whitetail hunting world are happening *right now.*

Never before have whitetails been as abundant and as accessible to so many. And if big bucks interest you, a quick perusal of either the Pope and Young or the Boone and Crockett Record Book will quickly convince you that the time for trophy bucks has not passed you by. Rather, we are in the midst of the best trophy whitetail hunting North

America's legions of deer hunters have ever enjoyed.

So come along while we take a look at hunting North America's most abundant and most popular big game animal, the white-tailed deer. If you are just getting started in this addictive sport, there is plenty of solid information in these pages which you can take right to the woods and put to work this season. And if you are a seasoned veteran, well, read on. I'm betting there's a tip or trick here that even you have not used and that you can put to good use wherever it is you hunt—big timber, farmland, riverbottom, prairie or anywhere in between.

Author Gary Clancy with a good farmland buck, taken with a muzzleloader. Before you load up or even step out the door, consider rutting conditions, weather and hunting pressure. These factors provide answers to the "how" and "where" of your hunting day.

RUT, WEATHER, HUNTING PRESSURE: 3 KEYS

Pre-rut, rut or post-rut? Hot, cold, windy, calm, wet or dry? Hunting pressure a factor? Answer these questions first before you ever begin trying to decide where, when and how to hunt white-tails. The timing of the rut, the weather, and hunting pressure are the three most important factors that should dictate when, where and how you hunt. Before I step out the door I want to know: What stage is the rut in? What's the weather like and what is the forecast? And how many other hunters are going to be sharing the woods with me?

Given this information, I can begin to formulate a hunting plan before I ever step foot in the woods.

Nine times out of ten, that hunting plan will call for hunting from a stand. Why a stand? It has to do with those three senses we discuss in the sidebar "Understanding Whitetails" (page 12).

In almost all cases—gun, bow, early season, late season, rut or not—mobility is key. You'll probably need to spend as much time scouting as hunting ... and even be willing to move your stand around.

Sitting quietly on a stand with the wind in your favor is simply the best way to see deer, especially deer at close range. A whitetail's vision is geared to detecting motion, so a hunter sitting still as stone is unlikely to be spotted. And even a whitetail cannot hear what is not there. Sit still and you will make no noise. Play the wind and even a whitetail will not smell you. Most of the time, you are better off sitting still and letting the deer come to you.

But where to sit? That's the biggest question whitetail fanatics continually ask themselves. Unfortunately for us as hunters, that "where" is constantly changing. It is true that white-tailed deer are creatures of habit, but those habits have a way of changing with the seasons, the weather, the stage of the rut, food sources, water supply, hunting pressure, land use alterations and other variables.

If you are going to ensure that your stand is always positioned in the best location possible, you are going to have to spend at least as much time scouting as you do hunting. It is the only way I know to stay on top of the changes in the whitetail world. I know a lot of hunters who put up a stand and then hunt that stand the entire season. That might work if you only hunt a long weekend, but if you hunt for weeks or months, no one stand is going to produce action the entire season.

STANDS: WHAT TO LOOK FOR

A good deer stand is one that is located within range of a place where deer are likely to present an opportunity for a shot during legal hunting hours. Here are the ten best places I know for a stand:

Deer Trails

Most deer trails are made by deer moving between food sources and bedding cover. Many, but not all, are used season after season. I know of some which have been in use by deer for over 30 years. But the fact that a deer trail has been dug a foot deep into the side of a hill by a thousand hooves does not mean that you should sit there. Yes, deer use those trails each

Every deer trail looks good. But will the deer be using it during the time of day—and season of the year—you'll be hunting it? The author offers simple ways to find out (read on to page 14).

year, but not all year long. Remember that deer moving between food and cover make most deer trails. The bedding cover might remain fairly constant decade after decade, barring any major disruptions such as logging or another subdivision. But the food source to which the trail connects will probably be used by the deer for only a month or two, maybe only a few weeks, of the year.

Understanding Whitetails

The beauty and grace of the elegant whitetail fascinates everyone, whether they hunt or not. Fawns are born in May or June and weigh only 4 to 8 pounds. Their reddish coats are covered with white spots that help to hide them from predators, such as coyotes and free-running dogs. The red coat on both fawns and adult deer is replaced by the grayer, heavier and warmer winter coat as fall approaches.

A mature doe will stand about 30 inches high at the shoulder, a big buck about 40 inches. From nose to tail, the average whitetail will stretch out to about 6 feet, although I've seen big bucks longer than 8 feet. Weight varies considerably from region to region. In the Florida Keys, a buck might weigh only 50 pounds, and I've shot several in the southeast states and in South Texas that weighed just over 100 pounds. At the other extreme, in northern Canada where the whitetail subsist at the very northern edge of their range, I have taken two bucks that each weighed more than 350 pounds on the hoof.

Part of the reason deer have adapted to such a wide range of climates and habitats is the fact that their four-part stomach allows them to eat, digest and live on just about any living vegetation. In

A big, mature doe is the matriarch of a whitetail clan. Young whitetails follow her lead in learning to be evasive.

South Texas for instance, where other food can be scarce during drought years, deer make do with prickly pear cactus. How they are able to take a bite without getting a mouthful of thorns is beyond me.

A whitetail is built for short bursts of speed, although he or she can trot for miles if need be. When startled, a buck can hit 40 mph for a short distance, and clear an 8-foot-high fence with ease. While hunting with a muzzleloader once, I slipped up on a dandy 8-point buck only to have my percussion cap fail to ignite. The buck nailed me when the hammer clicked. When I tried the cap again, the buck exploded as only a whitetail can explode. He covered 27 feet—I measured it—with his first leap. And that was from a standing start. Amazing.

But for all their speed, whitetails would usually rather slink and skulk than run. Whitetails, especially mature animals (bucks and does alike), have nerves of titanium. For every whitetail that flags its tail and waves good-bye to you, just figure that you have walked right past twice as many. This is because a mature whitetail—doe or buck—has an established home range, and it is within this area that the deer feels most secure. The size of the home range will vary from region to region, depending upon the habitat, but invariably does will have smaller home ranges than mature bucks, and the home range of a mature buck will typically overlap the home areas of four or more doe-family units. The importance of this information will surface when we discuss rut-hunting tactics in this chapter.

Whitetails are creatures of the edge—which is the zone between two types of habitat, or perhaps vegetation of different age. Common examples are the edge created where a crop field meets a woods, the banks of a stream or the boundaries of a clear cut. The conjunction of a wetland and a forest also creates an edge. But less obvious edge is just as important. A fenceline separating pastured forest from the thicker timber (which has not been pastured) is not an obvious edge and most hunters will overlook it, but I guarantee the deer will be traveling along that seam. Look for these "soft" edges too.

The whitetail's senses of sight, hearing and smell have been honed to near perfection as the species has evolved. Hunters commonly complain about a lack of deer in the area they are hunting, but the truth is that usually the deer are there all right, it is just that the deer are doing what whitetails do best ... using their senses to avoid contact with hunters.

In the vision department, white-tailed deer do not possess the binocular-like orbs of the pronghorn or wild sheep, but then they have no need for long-range optics. Without getting into the scientific jargon, suffice it to say that a whitetail sees much better in darkness and dim light than you and I do and is a master at detecting the slightest movement. Be still and a whitetail will not see you, but move and he will

nail you every time.

When it comes to hearing, those big ears are not just for looks. Like twin radar screens, those ears are constantly rotating to pick up sounds from any direction. And because a whitetail can move each ear individually, the animal has the capability to listen to more than one sound at once. A deer pinpoints the source of a sound due to the slight difference in time it takes for the sound to reach each individual ear. In my experience, deer are not quite as good at pinpointing the source of a sound as are predators or wild turkeys, but they ain't too shabby either! Most certainly, their skill here is exceptional enough to pinpoint a clumsy and loud hunter (which is all of us, to a deer!).

But it is that nose which usually beats us hunters. The whitetail's sense of smell cannot even *begin* to be fathomed by us humans. Consider that one-third of the whitetail's brain is devoted to recognizing various odors and then interpreting each of those odors. And beneath the skin of that black, shiny nose are nasal chambers that allow the whitetail to take the tiniest particle of scent and concentrate that scent so that the brain can better determine what the smell means. Is it food? Is it a predator? Is it man? Or can it be ignored? The answer is quick in coming and the deer reacts accordingly. Oh yes, did I mention that the whitetail can perform this function with six different odors all at once?

Researchers are just beginning to give us an understanding of how the whitetail sense of smell functions. The more I learn about the whitetail's sense of smell (and his other senses), the more I am amazed and the better I understand how the whitetail so easily evades hunters.

Full alert! With eyes, ears and nose operating at full speed, this lopsided but nice buck won't blunder into any fidgety, loud or scent-ignoring hunter.

An easy way to monitor deer traffic on a specific trail is to take a branch and smooth out a yard or two of the trail with sand or dirt. The number of tracks in the dirt a day or two later will reveal whether the trail is currently in use. The direction of the tracks will tell you if the deer are using the trail to move from cover to feed in the evening, to return to cover in the morning, or both. Or today you can even go high-tech and hang a monitoring device along the trail.

Most of the time, the closer you can hunt to the bedding area without disturbing the bedding area itself, the better your odds of catching a deer using the trail during daylight hours. However, as we will see in a moment, there are exceptions to that rule, just as there are exceptions to every "rule" when it comes to white-tailed deer.

Here's another tip that has paid off handsomely for me many times: When I find a good trail I walk its entire length, paying special attention to any place where another trail intersects with or crosses it. Hang a stand at this junction and you have just doubled your odds of seeing deer.

Food Sources

Sometimes it pays to hunt the food source itself. Usually the best spot is where the trail from the bedding cover enters the field.

There are three times of the year when hunting a field edge can pay off. One is early in archery season while deer are still in their late-summer pattern in which bucks still enter the fields with plenty of shooting light left. The second time period to consider a field-edge stand is during the peak of the breeding season, when bucks are searching for does. Bucks know which fields the does like to feed in, so they will cruise right through, or more commonly sneak just inside cover along the perimeter of the field to check for the presence of any does. The third time when a field-edge stand can produce is late in the season when deer are forced to feed earlier in the day because of snow, cold weather conditions and depleted food sources.

Funnels

Any time man-made or natural features severely restrict lateral deer movement, you have a funnel. If

Despite what you might otherwise read, there are times when it pays to hunt food field edges. Try this in the early season, while deer (like this Florida buck) are still in their summer patterns.

tracks, trails and droppings reveal that deer are indeed passing through such a pinch-point, put a stand there; it is one of the most dependable locations in the woods.

Saddles

A whitetail will take the easy way whenever possible and that is what makes a saddle on a steep ridge such a good place for a stand. Instead of climbing up and over the crest of a high ridge the deer will naturally use the easier "dip" of the saddle. The longer and steeper the ridge, the better a saddle will be.

Pressure Points

During most firearm deer seasons, the first few days of the season find the woods crawling with hunters. This is the time to use that hunting pressure to your advantage. The easiest way to do this is to determine where the pressure originates and the direction of movement of the bulk of the hunters, then position yourself in the way of deer slipping away from them. Usually this means getting up a little earlier and walking a little farther than other hunters, but it is the best way I know to tag a buck when the pressure is on. Locate the nastiest, wettest, thickest cover you can find beyond the range of the majority of hunters and you have yourself a winning stand site any time hunting pressure is a major factor in determining deer movement.

Rub Lines

Hunting rub lines is an early-season proposition, almost always a bowhunting situation. The best bucks in any given area make the earliest rubs. Find these rubs and you can bet you are hunting a good buck. The most common place to find early-season rubs is along the trail the buck is using to move from bedding to feeding cover. Besides tracks in the trail, you can often use the rub itself to determine which way the buck was headed when he made the rub. If the rubbed side of the sapling is facing the bedding area, odds are good the rub was made as the buck was heading to feed in the evening. But if

Figuring out when a rub line is being used is not a mystery. A rub facing the bedding area was probably made as the buck traveled out to feed in the evening. A rub facing the food source was probably made in the morning as the buck headed back to his daytime bed.

the bare bark is facing the food source, the rub was made in the morning. This knowledge will help you determine the best time to hunt each rub line.

Scrapes

Hunting over scrapes has been blown all out of proportion. When some hunters find a fresh scrape, or better yet a whole string of fresh pawings, they get all excited and hang a stand at the spot. Most of the time they never see the buck that made the scrapes. Why? Several reasons. One, most scrapes are made and checked at night.

Two, many scrapes are never revisited. And three, hunting over scrapes is only an effective tactic for a week to ten days or the season—those days immediately preceding the availability of estrous does when the bucks are super-ready but the ladies aren't. Many hunters continue to hunt over scrapes long after bucks have forgotten about them. If you are going to hunt over scrapes, here are my recommendations:

- **Concentrate on hunting the scrapes during the ten days preceding the actual breeding period of the rut.** If you don't know when this is, ask your local big game biologist. Prior to those ten days and after, forget about hunting scrapes.

- **Doctor the scrapes with plenty of scent.** Use a scent dripper over the scrape, or add scent to a baby food jar or film canister with holes punched in the lid, and then bury the container just under the surface of the dirt in a scrape.

This will encourage bucks to pay repeat visits. Put your stand on the downwind side of the scrapes. Bucks, especially mature animals, will often scent-check scrapes from downwind.

- **Do a lot of calling and rattling.** Picture a buck lying in his bed somewhere within a few hundred yards of where you sit hunting his scrape line. That buck might be content to lie there and chew his cud all day, leaving you watching squirrels and birdies. But if he hears what might be another buck grunting along his scrape line or a couple of bucks fighting, there is a good chance that he will get out of bed and come to investigate.

- **Use a decoy.** A buck decoy works best because it can trigger an aggressive reaction.

Left: If you're going to hunt a scrape line—it does work when the time is right—use scent to doctor the one you're hunting near. Above: Always imagine that the buck is very close, then sneak into his scrape line and call or rattle to get him up and moving toward you.

Shotguns for Whitetails

I grew up in a shotgun-only area. When my buddies and I went to the range to "sight in" our shotguns for the deer season, we didn't take paper targets, we took grocery boxes. The biggest we could find! If you could hit an empty cardboard box three out of five shots at 50 yards, you were ready. If not, you just kept getting bigger boxes.

Today's "slug guns" are, as the saying goes, "a whole different ball game." The biggest change? The rifled barrel. Put some spin on a projectile and it flies truer. When you match a rifled slug barrel with a saboted slug, you've got yourself a winning combination. Now top the shotgun off with a low-power scope, something in the 2X to 5X class, and you have yourself a lay-'em-down-for-keeps deer getter that is the equal of most rifles at ranges up to about 100 yards. After that, a shotgun slug drops like a well-centered goose.

Some shotgun hunters curse the new saboted slugs, claiming that accuracy with the new slugs is much worse than with the old Foster style slugs. In most cases this is because they are shooting the saboted slugs out of smoothbore barrels. In most smoothbores, the old Foster style slugs shoot better than the saboted slugs, but in rifled barrels the opposite is generally true.

Carefully sighted in, with a rifled barrel and a good low-power scope, a slug gun is as good as any high-powered rifle out to a hundred yards. NAHC staffer Jeff Boehler proved that with this incredible Iowa buck.

Hunt Chase Sign

As soon as bucks begin chasing does, you should be hunting "chase sign." If there is snow on the ground, evidence of bucks chasing does is easy to see, but in the leaves it takes some experience to spot. Just look for areas where the leaves are freshly turned in a maze of unpredictable patterns. The sign is easiest to spot on hillsides. Hang a stand and hunt there right now, because these areas only stay "hot" for a day or two, but the amorous pair may come right back through on one of their love jaunts.

Crossings

Look for places where deer cross a deep gully, a creek, a river or a fence. Remember, deer are creatures of habit and if you can find a place where they are in the habit of crossing any obstruction, you have found yourself a very dependable stand location. You can encourage deer to cross a fence at a specific location by wiring the top two strands of fence together. Be sure you have the permission of the landowner.

When the bucks are interested in breeding, leave the scrapes and hunt those places where the bucks chase does. The deer will cover a lot of territory, and there's a decent chance they'll come right back through.

With landowner permission, you can encourage deer to cross at a specific point: Just twist the top two strands of a fence together. Both bucks and does will gravitate to the easy slip-through spot.

Bedding Areas

I've saved this one for last because hunting the bedding area should be last on your list of stand locations. No, you won't force a deer to permanently vacate a bedding area by disturbing him a time or two, but if the deer sense that you have become a permanent bother, they will go elsewhere. If you are going to hunt a bedding area, resign yourself to an all-day sit. Get to the stand in the dark before any deer arrive at the bedding area and plan to stay all day; do not leave until after the deer have left in the evening. That way you won't spook deer coming or going. And try to stay awake from 11 a.m. until 2 p.m. Sometime during this three-hour period deer will get up out of their beds to stretch, relieve themselves and grab a quick snack. The buck or doe you've been waiting for might mosey past.

DEER DRIVES

When deer are not moving on their own, either naturally or because of hunting pressure, you have three choices: get together with buddies and do some deer drives; do a little still-hunting; or go home and catch up on those honey-do's. The honey-do list will still be there when deer season's over, so I say hunt. We'll cover still-hunting next, so let's discuss deer drives here.

Deer drives that involve "gangs" of hunters are usually a real fiasco. These drives take too long to develop, someone is always out of position, and most of the deer just slip out to the side or back through the haphazard line of drivers. The best drives are ones that use two to six hunters concentrating on small, manageable parcels of cover.

You don't need, or want, a huge gang to drive deer. Even two hunters—working together well in country they know—can make effective drives, as evidenced here.

Muzzleloading for Whitetails

Load up (left) with 100 grains of Pyrodex (two 50-grain pellets) and a 240- to 300-grain saboted bullet. You'll be deadly from point-blank range out to 130 yards. Simple, effective and proven muzzleloader advice: Opt for an in-line rifle (below) where legal.

*U*nless you have a real hankering to go the authentic route for nostalgic reasons, buy yourself a good in-line rifle. An in-line is the most dependable of all of the ignition types. I can tell you from a number of sad experiences that there are few things more disheartening than to hunt well and hard and then miss an opportunity at a good buck because the damn gun does not go off when you pull the trigger. With an in-line, misfires are rare and when they do occur it is almost always human error and not the fault of the rifle.

I've got two in-line muzzleloaders. One has fiber-optic open sights which I use when hunting in states that still have laws against scopes for use on muzzleloaders during special muzzleloader seasons. The other sports a 2X-7X variable scope. I load both with two Pyrodex pellets (the pellets are 50 grains each) and a 240- to 300-grain saboted bullet, specifically designed to mushroom at velocities achieved with muzzleloading rifles. Nosler, Winchester, Remington, Barnes, Swift, Speer and others all make premium bullets for use in muzzleloaders. Both my rifles are designed to take up to a 150-grain charge of either Pyrodex or blackpowder. But I've found that accuracy suffers in my rifles when I boost the charge much beyond 100 grains. Sighted in to be dead-on at 100 yards I can hold on the chest at anything from in-my-face to 130 yards.

When planning drives, choose small parcels of cover—even tiny patches. Remember: If you have to drive deer, they're probably under pressure from all fronts, so try oddball spots and places "close" to civilization (where you can still shoot safely and legally).

Here are the keys to successful deer drives:

- **Do your drives at midday, when deer are most likely to be bedded in the cover being driven. Choose your cover wisely.** Strips or small parcels of cover are easier to drive than a big block of cover. Think thick, nasty and wet. Those are the places deer bed, especially when the pressure is on. And as the old adage goes, don't bite off more than you can chew. You can't move deer along a whole mountainside, but you and your buddy can effectively push that brushy draw, skinny creekbottom, tiny woodlot or grassy swale.

- **Give the standers plenty of time to get in position.** If you think it will take them 10 minutes, give them 20 instead. Make sure that standers do not get to their stands by walking through the area to be driven. Sounds elementary I know, but a lot of drives are over before they ever start because the standers bumble through or near the cover and flush the deer before the hunt ever begins.

- **In thick cover, like cattails for instance, drivers should walk ten steps and stop.** Pause for about 20 seconds and then start walking again. That stop-and-go will unnerve deer that otherwise would hold tight and let you walk right by. In almost all cases, this silent technique will work better than any hoot-n-holler scenario, where every deer in the county will know exactly where every hunter is and react accordingly, squirting out where you don't want them to.

- **Drivers should go through the thickest patches of cover, rather than skirting them.** A whitetail will sit incredibly tight, and a lazy driver meandering down the easiest route won't roust many deer.

This buck isn't going anywhere when a lazy, nonchalant driver meanders through. Drivers have to hit the thick stuff like they're trying to kick out big white-tailed bunnies!

- **Know how to use the wind.** The general rule is for drivers to move into cover with the wind at their backs so that their scent disperses into cover and helps to move deer. Also, the moving deer won't smell and avoid the standers as easily.

- **One safety rule:** Drivers should *never* shoot in the direction of standers and vice versa, no matter how big the buck.

Archery Gear for Whitetails

Most bowhunters are better off with a compound bow than a recurve or longbow. It takes less time and less practice to become proficient with a compound bow—especially one set up with sights, peep and a mechanical release—than it does with a recurve or longbow.

As long as I've already upset my traditionalist friends, I might as well go all the way and take on the "speed freaks" too. A lot of bowhunting writers and editors fit into this category, so magazines are full of stories about speed. Light arrows, light mechanical broadheads, overdraws and radical high-energy cams are all the rage. On the 3-D course, all this speed will help you win tournaments, but in the field, the same equipment will cost you.

Broadheads tend to fly best at speeds of 250 feet per second (fps) or less. In fact, part of the popularity of mechanical broadheads is due to the fact that archers could not get fixed-blade heads to fly decently out of their high-speed bows. A compound achieving moderate speed is also quieter than a faster bow. This is important. If an animal hears the bow, it can easily jump the string. Those who promote speed will often say that with a "screaming" arrow the deer does not have time to jump the string. Hogwash! Check out the speed of sound sometime and then see how that 300 fps stacks up!

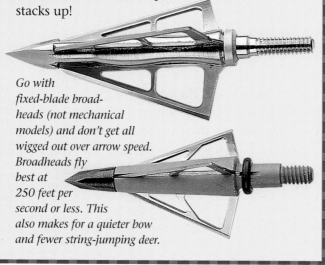

Go with fixed-blade broadheads (not mechanical models) and don't get all wigged out over arrow speed. Broadheads fly best at 250 feet per second or less. This also makes for a quieter bow and fewer string-jumping deer.

When sneak-hunting, wait and watch more than you walk.

SNEAK-HUNTING (STILL-HUNTING)

It's called still-hunting, but this is my chapter, so let's use "sneak-hunting" instead, because that term better describes this tactic.

There are very few good sneak hunters. The reason for this: Sneak-hunting, when done correctly, is the most mentally demanding of all of the whitetail hunting tactics. A lot of hunters go for a walk in the woods when they get tired of sitting on stand and call it still-hunting, but only a handful really sneak-hunt.

An accomplished sneak hunter might cover the length of a football field in an hour or two. That takes patience. A good sneak hunter will never take more than a handful of steps without stopping to look and listen. An accomplished sneak hunter is stationary much more than he is moving.

I once spent four hours sneaking through a stand of thick aspens that was no more than 200 yards long by 50 yards wide. Six inches of new wet snow lay underfoot and even this 200-pound Irishman could move without sound. I was on my knees peering under the snow-laden branches when the buck appeared. He dropped seven feet from the twin dimples my knees left in the snow.

You cannot sneak-hunt effectively unless conditions are perfect. That means quiet footing. Wet snow is ideal. You can forget about slipping up on a whitetail with crusted snow. Leaves wet from rain or melted frost will work. And a little wind to cover any sounds you may make will help; plus that wind helps you determine a hunt path to keep your scent from the deer. One of the biggest mistakes would-be sneak hunters make is attempting to sneak-hunt at midday, when most deer are bedded down. The best times to sneak-hunt are when deer are up and moving, early and late in the day.

SPOT-&-STALK HUNTING

Spot-and-stalk hunting is usually reserved for sheep, goats, mule deer and pronghorns. But whitetail? Granted, it does not happen often, but if you hunt whitetails long enough and in varied habitats, you will encounter places and situations where spot-and-stalk is the way to go. In fact, even as I pen these words, I just returned from the Milk River in northeastern Montana, where I took a dandy 10-point buck by employing spot-and-stalk tactics. Like the other times when I have had the opportunity to spot and then stalk, this stalk was not planned, it just happened that the buck was not going to come by my treestand, and he happened to be in a position where I thought I could slip within range of him. Don't count on spotting and stalking as a main tactic, but when the oppor-

tunity presents itself, go for it. [Editor's note: Spot-and-stalk tactics discussed in other chapters of this book, including mule deer and pronghorn, will also work on whitetails, where the terrain permits.]

Spot-and-stalk techniques can work on whitetails whether you have bow (left) or rifle (above) in hand.

EVERYONE'S DEER

Whether you hunt them in the North, South, East or West—in farmland fields and woodlots, deep timber, swamps, riverbottoms, hills or maybe even mountains—whitetails are truly everyone's deer. While they may seem common (and I guess you could say they are in this day and age), they are also extraordinary.

There is, quite possibly, no other animal as elusive as a mature whitetail. That goes for both bucks and does. Hunting them isn't rocket science, but it is hard work … and an exercise in taking care of details and *respecting* their incredible senses.

Entire books are written about whitetails and hunting them, so there's no way a chapter of this size can cover everything. But the strategies, techniques and tips I've outlined should help you on your quest to be more successful, more often, on hunts for your deer, everyone's deer—our beautiful and wonderful whitetail. 🦌

Rifles for Whitetails

Rifles ... when I was a kid, back in the '60s, every deer hunter I knew was convinced that calibers like the .30-30 Winchester and .35 Remington were (because of their large, comparatively slow-moving bullets) the best option for hunting deer in heavy cover. The myth back then was that these "brush busters" would bore right through the bramble and branches, and those lighter, faster bullets from speed demons (like the .243 and .270) would "blow up" on contact with a branch or deflect off the tiniest twig. This made these calibers better suited for mule deer and antelope, species more often found in wide-open places.

The sad part is that the same myth rampant 30 years ago refuses to die. It is kept alive in deer camps all across North America by hard-nosed hunters refusing to believe the results of numerous tests that prove there is no such thing as a "brush buster" bullet or caliber.

The truth of the matter is that no matter what caliber you choose, if you insist on trying to punch through screens of cover, deflections are going to occur. Interestingly, research on projectile deflection has proven that some of the worst offenders when it came to deflections were the big, round-nosed, slower-moving projectiles that some hunters continue to call "brush busters."

When it comes to rifle action type, it really is a matter of your own personal taste. At one time, there were more lever-action rifles in the woods than any other type; but today, bolt actions far outdistance all other actions combined. There is a reason for the popularity of bolt actions: They are strong, reliable, and—with a little practice—as fast at delivering a quick, well-placed follow-up shot as any other action, including the semiautomatic.

Caliber and bullet selection are far more important than brand name, action-type, stock material or any cosmetic considerations. Here are my top five picks:

Caliber: .25-06   Bullet: 120 grain

I've shot a bunch of deer with a .25-06. The only one that ever required a second round was a Wisconsin buck and that was my fault. I mixed up some handloads and mistakenly went hunting that day with some really hot 90-grain pills I had intended for coyotes. The .25-06 is a very accurate round, features flat trajectory, and because of its very mild recoil, would be my first choice for a young hunter or anyone who is recoil sensitive.

Caliber: .270   Bullet: 130 grain

You can't mention the .270 without breathing the words Jack O'Connor in the same breath. This was Jack's baby and his writing always gets the credit for making the .270 what it is. But the truth is that the .270 would have found its place in the ranks of the world's greatest calibers with or without

North, South, East or West—for a whitetail rifle, you can't go wrong with a solid bolt action mounted with a good low-power or variable scope. And a bolt can deliver follow-up shots as quickly as any other action, so don't feel disadvantaged there.

All your planning and hard work comes down to one fleeting opportunity. Don't "over-scope" yourself. Shoot often. Sight in carefully. Be confident so you can take a good shot when the buck is there. He won't stand around forever!

Jack O'Connor. Jack just escalated the process. The .270 is another good choice for anyone who is concerned about recoil but does not want to sacrifice anything on the other end.

Caliber: .280   Bullet: 140 grain

If the .280 had been around, it would have been O'Connor's baby. It does everything the .270 can do and then some.

Caliber: 7mm-08   Bullet: 140 grain

Very accurate, mild recoil and everything you will ever need for white-tailed deer. This round, which is nothing more than a .308 that has been necked down to 7mm, is a favorite with a couple of the best rifle hunters I know.

Caliber: .30-06   Bullet: 165 grain

What can you say about a caliber that has been laying out whitetail and winning wars since 1906? With today's fodder the '06 is not only one fine whitetail rifle, but with the right load it is up to the task of taking any game animal on this continent.

Rifle Scope Notes

The trend today in rifle scopes is to make them bigger and more powerful than the competition's. There may be a place for these optics, but the whitetail woods is not one of them. I've been hunting deer long enough to have earned a spot with the gray-beards and in all of those years I cannot think of one instance when I could have used 12, 16 or 25X.

For deer hunting I like a compact, variable scope with a low end below 3X. My two favorites are variables of a 1.5X6 and 2X7. Oh yes, and I always have the scope set at the lowest magnification. I wish I had a ten-dollar bill for every time I heard a disgruntled hunter come into camp and say something like, "I was just walking back to camp for lunch when this big buck busted out of a briar patch not 30 feet away. When I tried to get on him, I couldn't find him in my scope." When you've got a variable cranked up to anything over about 5X, getting on a moving deer at close range, especially in heavy cover, is nearly impossible. If you do find him in the glass at say 9X, all you are going to see is a blur of gray. And that's nothing to shoot at.

Chapter 2

COUES' DEER: HUNTING THE TOUGHEST WHITETAIL

BY PATRICK MEITIN

For my money, the diminutive Coues' white-tailed deer of southwest New Mexico, Old Mexico and southern Arizona is the toughest, sportiest big game quarry around.

The Southwest's little whitetail goes by many labels. In much of Arizona, he is simply called whitetail or fantail. More commonly he is called "Coose" or "Cooze" deer, but this is more correctly pronounced "Cows" after namesake Dr. Elliot Coues. Dr. Coues first scientifically described the species while he was an Army field doctor during the 1870s.

You may also hear names that can't be printed here, for the most part from flabbergasted nimrods foiled repeatedly by this Einsteinian deer of the desert. Hunters of no less experience than Jack O'Connor proclaimed Coues' the toughest game on Earth. This recognition would have been impressive enough had O'Connor remained in his home state of Arizona, but the man hunted across the continent and globe, bagged mountain sheep galore, and shot African game from antelope to zebra. Operate in prime Coues' habitat, and you too will come to believe a good Coues' buck is the toughest game on Earth.

It's not enough to hunt in the very best habitat, though that is much of the Coues' hunting equation. Nor is it sufficient to be more condi-tioned than the average hunter and be able to traipse through Coues' country all day, though this too is all-important. To tag Coues' with any amount of regularity you must hunt smart.

The Coues' is cloaked in a coat of slate gray, allowing him to slip into shadow like a wraith, and his tiny 90-pound dimensions allow him to skulk beside your average covey of desert quail.

Right: Author Patrick Meitin toting out a good-sized Coues' buck. Be ready for rough country and hard work, or stay home! The deer's diminutive size makes him hard to find, to be sure, but look at that gray coat as well.

You'll spot many Coues' bucks like this, glimpsed in a patch of open ground surrounded by thick vegetation (here, mountain mahogany, Coues' favorite food). Get a fix on his location before you look away, because he'll move and be hard to find again.

His wary demeanor nearly always keeps him one step ahead too. All this secrecy and evasiveness has nothing to do with human hunting pressure. The Coues' happens to be a delicacy among stealthy desert predators. In a climate like this, where meat is always in short supply, you become neurotic or you are eaten.

Perhaps you have not heard much about this challenging big game animal, although this is unlikely considering today's rush for "slams" of various species. More likely you have heard a few things but know little of this tiny and beautiful whitetail subspecies. Why should these whitetail runts interest you? Challenge mostly: They are tough to get. To a lesser extent the variety they offer is incentive enough to come hunt them; few hunters have ever shot a Coues' deer. But as much as anything, the change of scenery, the country these deer bring you to, is the major draw. The desert Southwest gets in your blood!

WHERE TO FIND COUES' DEER

Found only in the extreme southwest corner of New Mexico, the southern third of Arizona and the Mexican states of Sonora, western Chihuahua and northern Sinaloa, the Coues' is a denizen of dry places. He can survive long periods without water, absorbing dew from vegetation and the juices of his browse. This is a land of thorn and cactus, extremes in temperatures, and boot-sole-shredding rocks with edges like serrated knives. It is a stark yet lovely land that will break you quickly if you're not prepared.

Arizona hunters enjoy the Coues' as a mainstay, a yearly ritual when the lottery drawing system affords the lucky hunter a permit. More often than not, a permit does arrive. Romantic names of ancient places flow off these hunters' tongues as they formulate plans: Galiuros, Patagonias, Pinalenos, Dragoons, Sierra Anchas, San Carlos Apache Indian Reservation, and more.

This incredible Coues' from Old Mexico far surpasses the Boone and Crockett 110-inch minimum, and the cheaters and rare drop point make it one of the most beautiful Coues' bucks the author has ever guided a hunter to.

New Mexico hunters are becoming more Coues' savvy all the time, so much so that the Peloncillo Mountains—once *the* hot spot—has since gone to limited-draw permits. Locations such as Alamo Huecos, the San Francisco Mountains and Mule Creek have replaced the Peloncillos as hot spots.

And then there is Mexico. There may be no better place to tag an outsized Coues' buck today, but Mexico has a long history of corruption. There are many palms to grease, and a native outfitter is required by law. You do not hunt on your own south of the border, and hunts start at $3,500.

GLASSING UP A BUCK

You can get a buck on your own, stateside. Day-in and day-out, probing with powerful optics is your best bet for success on Coues' whitetails. Nearly all Coues' territory is tilted severely, so even in thickly vegetated areas, ferreting game from opposing hillsides with powerful glass is feasible.

Now there is glassing, and there is *glassing.* Watch the average hunter sweep binoculars randomly across distant hillsides and you wonder why he carries the optics at all. In Coues' hunting you must learn to see with your binoculars, not simply through them.

When you're not hiking around rocky and severely tilted terrain, you'll be glassing for Coues' bucks. And glassing. And glassing some more. Mount good 15X60 binoculars on a tripod for maximum steadiness and minimum eyestrain.

Understanding Coues' Deer

No other North American big game animal is as wonderfully camouflaged as a Coues' deer. Both bucks and does are grayer- and lighter-colored than their bigger white-tailed cousins to the north and east. You can practically go blind trying to pick out a Coues' against the backdrop of his gray-sandy-rocky desert habitat.

Coues' deer are the symbol of whitetail adaptability. Living in desert mountains, they make a living in some awfully harsh places. Coues' like steep, rough, broken country … places usually not suitable for cattle or even mule deer. Unlike other whitetails, Coues' seem to like some elevation, and you'll find most from 3,900 to 7,800 feet. Vegetation in Coues' country is always brushy, thorny, cactusy and sharp; rough stuff too.

Water is key to Coues' survival, and may well be the limiting factor in where a Coues' deer can live. Riparian (stream-side) habitat used to be key, but so much of that has been tamed or plain-out settled by man, that Coues' deer have been relegated to fragment

This is a good, mature Coues' buck. No, his antlers aren't as big as some Canadian behemoth, but this little desert Coues' whitetail is handsome, and may quite well be North America's toughest hunting trophy.

pieces of habitat off the beaten path, where no one wants to live or try to eke out a living.

Water also dictates a Coues' deer's feeding strategy throughout the year. In spring (when rainfall is at its peak) grasses, forbs and new leaves and twigs account for most of the forage. But as the land parches in late summer and autumn, Coues' deer become browsers; mountain mahogany is a favorite.

Coues' deer are North America's smallest hoofed big game (a good buck will weigh 100 to 125 pounds, and a doe will weigh more like 80 pounds) … but they are a BIG hunting challenge. Any Coues' buck is a good one, and you will work long and hard to shoot one.

Choosing Glass

By binoculars I mean quality glass. Look to Germany and 10X40 packages, or the best Japanese and American labels you can possibly afford. Zeiss, Leica and Bausch & Lomb are industry touchstones. If it doesn't hurt to scratch out the check or add to the credit card balance, dig even deeper. Cheap binoculars are great migraine inducers, and are guaranteed to become useless within a few short seasons. The worst

thing of all about cheap binoculars: You won't use them as often, which means you can't be hunting as hard or spotting many (or any) animals.

Accept nothing short of gin-clearness and rugged longevity in your binoculars.

Most dead-serious Coues' hunters also own a pair of German 15X60 binoculars. These prove invaluable, mounted atop a tripod. Stock-still there on the tripod, these high-magnification optics cut both distance and shadow to reveal trophy Coues' bucks in faraway cover.

While you're at it, you really do need a spotting scope. Even if you're not hunting for a book buck, the increased magnification carries you painlessly across chasms and rockslides for a closer look at something that could be only a doe, or a soft-looking rock, or a buck.

So you've spent the necessary dollars and you've got good glass; here's how to use it efficiently.

How to Glass

Gaining the high ground and a commanding view are paramount to effective glassing for Coues' bucks. Invite a buddy along to enjoy the fun too—that never hurt a thing, and the more eyes the better.

Set up your 15-power binoculars and spotting scope as first light arrives. When enough light has arrived, use your 10X40s or 8X35s to check obvious places where deer might be up and moving.

After dissecting an area carefully—reading the terrain painstakingly with slow left-to-right or up-and-down panning—double-check the entire scene with the bigger 15s. Give shaded bushes and trees, and disguising cuts and gullies, special attention.

Dismiss nothing. Investigate anything appearing out of place, with your spotting scope. That lump you've just discovered could be only a weathered stump … or it could be the buck of a lifetime. Abandon your perch only when you're certain you've missed nothing. This could take hours.

DO YOUR SCOUTING

Preseason scouting is an important mental aspect in the Coues' game. How? Scouting makes you confident and keeps you at task during those tedious hours when your trophy does not appear.

Sure evidence of a good buck in the area can keep your spirits up and your eyes to the glass. Small cloven-hoof prints and ball-bearing-sized

Coues' bucks are quite territorial, meaning that you'll likely find a summer velvet buck like this near the same spot when the season opens. So scout hard. And then when you hunt, don't give up: Work hard and be confident that the bucks you found before are still around.

Two buddies with a pair of 10X40 binoculars, a tripod-mounted 15X60 and spotting scope at-the-ready make a great team in Coues' country. The simple rule for glassing: Dismiss nothing, investigate everything.

droppings are a beginning. Shed antlers are even better, providing insight to the trophy potential of an area. A Coues' whitetail buck, unless unduly harassed or subjected to abnormal weather, will seldom roam out of a single square mile home range, except, possibly, during the rut in December and January. Find an impressive shed and you're well on your way to trophy success!

COUES' FIELD JUDGING KNOW-HOW

Any Coues' buck is a good one, and just hunting the magnificent desert country is reward itself. But because Coues' deer are so limited in their availability and range, most first-time Coues' hunters don't know a great buck when they see him.

Judging Coues' bucks on the hoof for the record book is trickier than it might initially appear. First, mere inches here and there can mean the difference between a so-so buck and a real trophy. Deductions can add up quickly. Boone and Crockett has set 110 inches as the minimum for all-time records, 100 for awards recognition. Nearly any experienced Coues' hunter will agree a 100-inch buck is a darn fine animal. To most hunters any 4X4 (three points per side plus brow tines) is a shooter, no matter the dimensions. For the most part, this is true.

If you're determined to tag a super buck, you'll have to pass these tempting targets. In general, look

This is what a Boone and Crockett Coues' buck looks like, down to the inch. Tom Drumme took this beautiful 100-inch buck at 350 yards with a .25-06.

for about 12 inches of mass per side—translation, at least 4-inch bases—and beams that carry this mass well out toward the tips. Two tines as long as (or longer than) a buck's ears are important, as well as main beams that sickle out nicely to at least $2^1/_2$ times an ear's length. A mature Coues' buck's ear will measure 6 inches. Look for abnormalities that will come off as deductions. Seek a spread to at least the tips of the ears in a relaxed position.

Let's build the perfect book buck: We'll make him an 8-point, or 4X4. He will sport $18^1/_2$-inch main beams, no deductions. (Hey, why not?) And why not a 15-inch inside spread? We'll plug in our standard 12 inches of mass per side, say 4-inch C-1 (First circumference), $3^1/_2$-inch C-2, $2^1/_2$-inch C-3, which leaves 2 inches between the last point and beam tip. His brows are gorgeous, at 3 inches each. That leaves room for two 8-inch G-2s (second tine after brow), and another 6-inch tine per side. One hundred ten points. Of course, a buck without deductions does not exist, but you get the picture.

A 5X5 buck is rare, and a great majority of them will make book; in fact the highest scorers are often 5X5s. Not all, mind you, if tines are stubby or lacking mass.

You will often find Coues' bucks like this, bedded tight in midday cover. This is a nice buck that will score in the mid- to high 90s.

Author Meitin with a gorgeous Boone and Crockett buck. This rack has everything—long tines, sweeping main beams, mass, rare cheaters and even a drop point.

Any non-typical is worth taking a hard look at, as darn few are taken, with less than 50 total in the B&C records, opposed to more than 200 typical bucks.

Looking at photos of B&C Coues' bucks, or even mounted animals you may have access to, is the best teacher. Antler and body proportions are vastly different from those of Eastern whitetail bucks tallying the same scores, so they are not good bases to go on. The antlers aren't huge, even on a good buck, so be careful as you analyze but not overcautious!

Beware of bucks jumped from their beds and running straight away, as they always somehow look bigger than reality. The best view in my estimate is a good, long, side-on angle. This gives you an accurate idea of tine length, mass and main-beam length, the three most important factors when scoring a Coues' buck. Beware, too, of head-on views and extremely wide racks, as spread credit in excess of main-beam length is deducted from the final score.

MAKING THE STALK

A Coues' stalk by necessity is conducted carefully but swiftly. When a buck falls into shadow to bed, it's extremely difficult to locate him again, even at decent range. It is critical to mark key landmarks around your buck before stalking closer; identify some landmarks even before he beds.

The usual plan is to wait for the animal to bed if the terrain will allow a stalk. Generally, Coues' bed near 10 a.m., depending on weather, and remain there until noon. It's a shame to locate a buck after hard hunting only to lose him while making a move. Your hunting partner (remember him?) can help you close in too, using preestablished hand signals to direct you.

As you might have gathered, Coues' hunting is not for the weak of heart, the infirm or the impatient. A Coues' buck is one of North America's hardest-won trophies. He lives in truly wild, untamed country that will test *you* as much as your quarry. If you're tough enough, good enough, you just might collect your prize.

Coues' deer live in tough country. You have to be tough to hunt them successfully.

Equipment: Coues' Whitetail Firepower

There are two givens in Coues' hunting: Your target is small (though tough), and ranges can be quite long. Beyond these givens, little about Coues' hunting is certain. Thinking back on the very best Coues' bucks my clients have taken, I remember a 90-yard shot at a bedded 119-inch buck holed up beneath rim-rock. I also remember a beautiful 124 typical, and another 138 non-typical, dropped at close to 500 yards. (These were extremely long shots and probably shouldn't be attempted by most hunters.) Average these extremes and you're still talking 300 yards; that's not a slam dunk by any estimation!

Also, consider the rough-and-tumble nature of Coues' haunts, and choose a rifle you can carry comfortably during a long day afield. Today that means synthetic stocks. Custom guns of this class are expensive but ultra-accurate. You might also choose from a number of rifles offered by nearly all major manufacturers today: slimmed lines dropped into a light, accuracy-enhancing chassis. Aftermarket composite

stocks made to cradle your tried-and-true wood-stocked favorite are viable options.

If you want to begin a heated debate, mention caliber choice before a crowd of Coues' aficionados. The following calibers and loads are difficult to better: a .25-06, hot-loaded with a good 117-grain pill; the .270 throwing a heavier 130-grain slug for windy conditions; a 120-grain bullet in the reliable 7X57mm Mauser; or the .280 Remington spitting a 140-grain with more authority. If I've not named your favorite, don't despair, the numbers are nearly the same, and that's all that counts here. That .25 to .28 caliber range is about right.

There are all manner of super-charged belted magnums out there that also fill the bill today, from lesser-known makers to household names such as Weatherby; the .257 and .270 Weatherby Mags are particularly good Coues' calibers. These calibers flatten trajectory just a tad, and when situations become dicey there's a lot to be said about that.

Fans of bigger kick will choose a 7mm Mag. of some dimension, or even any number of .300 Mags, and there certainly is nothing wrong with any of these. You simply can't kill a Coues' too dead, and you have to hit them first. If a bigger gun will help you accomplish this, all the better.

The recent rage is artillery shells owning big cases and smaller bullets. I recently grassed a Boone and Crockett pronghorn at 486 steps, using a 7mm STW loaded with a 140-grain bullet at 3,600 fps. I became a great believer. Others include

Coues' whitetail hunting offers some of the trickiest shooting in the trade, with some shots taken at extreme ranges and many from odd angles. Be prepared with a flat-shooting rifle that you can carry all day, and finely honed shooting skills.

The only way you'll get to do the best work of all—packing out a good buck like this one—is by getting in shape so you can get to where the bucks are and by knowing your rifle so you can make the shot under challenging conditions.

the .300 Super Mag., .30-378 Weatherby Mag. and proprietary cartridges of certain custom rifle makers. When you get a good-sized chunk of lead moving at these speeds—some up to 4,000 fps—impressive things occur on the receiving end, even when ranges become ridiculous. Expect considerable recoil.

Action? Go for a bolt. It's accurate and reliable and you don't want to blow a good opportunity because of a jammed gun. The desert is a dusty, dirty place and the bolt will be a little forgiving. Today's single-shot rifles also could be good, especially from an accuracy standpoint.

The only advice I can offer on a rifle scope: Keep it rugged. Your model has to be able to take a few bumps and remain on zero. Make mine a straight 6X, though I know there are those who'll never use anything but a 3X9 or 4X12 variable. There's no single answer, only what you feel comfortable with. And don't skimp on scope mounts. Buy the best.

A great Coues' buck is a less-than-once-in-a-lifetime opportunity, which means if you see one, you probably have already invested a lot—of both money and time—preparing for this moment of truth. Be ready.

Rugged equipment, persistence and patience will help give you a chance to walk up to a superb Coues' buck like this one. This is the buck of a lifetime!

Chapter 3

ELK: HUNTING HARD, HUNTING SMART

BY JIM ZUMBO

A veteran hunter made a profound statement many years ago that I've never forgotten. He opined that elk were far and away the most difficult big game animals to hunt in North America. Since this man had hunted all around the world many times over, his credibility was as good as gold, but I had no clue what he was talking about. I hadn't yet experienced my first elk hunt, and could not comprehend his reasoning.

Now, some 35 years later, I know exactly where he was coming from. I hear myself repeating his words to others who have yet to experience the elk woods for the first time.

The immensity of the country sets elk hunting apart. Conquering steep, heavily timbered and often unroaded habitat comprises the biggest part of the elk hunting challenge.

THE BIGGEST CHALLENGE: BIG COUNTRY

There are some immensely important differences between elk and our other big game animals. If we sum up those variables, we can conclude that one element makes elk such a hunting challenge—the landscape. Elk country is like nothing else on the continent. Typically, you can count on the elk's domain as being steep, heavily timbered and largely unroaded. There are exceptions, of course, but those three scenarios are precisely why less than 20 percent of the elk hunters in America are successful each autumn.

It's commonly believed that elk have been in North America for only 10,000 years, crossing into

Packing in and staying awhile is often the only way to get into (and effectively hunt) truly good elk country.

Alaska from Siberia by walking across the land/ice bridge that is now the Aleutian Islands. Traveling southward as the Ice Age was nearing its conclusion, elk thrived in the same kind of country from whence they came—cold, mountainous regions with plenty of timber.

Obviously, the preferred habitat of elk is the undoing of most hunters who seek these big animals. Whereas you can outwit a huge whitetail buck in the back forty, only 200 yards from the barn, by learning his patterns, you can't and won't do the same with elk. Brawn, rather than brains, will undoubtedly be a critical factor in your quest, though hunting smart is certainly a mandatory requirement.

If you can't physically get to where elk are living, all else is in vain, pure and simple. Nothing

else is higher on the priority list. In typical elk country, you might need to travel several miles through dense forest, much of it uphill, to areas that elk are using. That necessity is the downfall of the hunter who isn't up to or interested in the task of accomplishing this serious and vital chore.

THREE ELK HUNTING "SEASONS"

Complicating the elk hunting picture is the mental aspect. Not only must you have the enthusiasm, perseverance and optimism to forge ahead, you must also understand the way an elk's brain works. You'll be hunting three completely different animals, depending on which of the three seasons you opt to hunt. Not only does the animal go through a serious transformation from late summer to late fall, but so do the mountains in which he lives. Elk and elk country intricately interact, requiring the hunter to make strategy adjustments as required.

In a nutshell, here's how elk behave, starting from the time the antlers are hardened. You'll also find hunting strategies and tactics that relate to the season at hand.

BUGLING SEASON

Bulls stay in bachelor groups all summer, but when their testosterone level increases and the velvet sluffs off their antlers, they begin reacting to the mating urge. Bulls become agitated with each other and leave their former male groups in search of cows. At that point they're on their own, gathering as many cows as they can into harems that they'll rule until the breeding season is over and every cow is bred. This is the first of the three seasons I've alluded to, commonly called the *bugling season*.

As you can imagine, this is a period of chaos in the elk woods. Crazed, lovesick bulls are tearing around, either keeping a harem intact or looking for unattached cows. This is the magical time of year that bulls bugle, piercing the high country with incredible screams that bring tears to the eyes of grown men. Few sounds in nature are as thrilling and exciting.

A bugling bull. The sound will make your heart beat triple time—because it's haunting and beautiful, but also because it means: Bull elk I can hunt!

Books have been written as to the subtleties of calling elk, but only experience will allow you to master the techniques. You need to see, smell and hear the elk woods during the famed rut, and work with bulls that may or may not cooperate.

Common sense as well as an understanding of elk communication is essential. For example, hunters who fail to call in a specific bull usually blame themselves, assuming they're calling incorrectly. Chances are good that you're doing just fine, but your bull is behaving normally if he's a herd bull with cows. Rather than charge in to pick a fight with you, whom he views as a competitor, he opts to waltz off with his ladies, preferring romance over battle.

And who can blame the big boy? After all, he's worked hard to gain his harem, possibly battling

One reality of bugling at a bull: He'll likely herd his cows over the ridge rather than come to you (a challenging bull) for a fight.

or bluffing other bulls. With only four weeks to mate, he's intent on doing just that. Fighting is not an attractive option, though some herd bulls are so mean and aggressive that they'll indeed temporarily leave their ladies to kick your butt. But don't count on it.

And how about the solo bull that has no girls waiting in the bushes? He's not at all interested in challenging your bugle cries, and in fact has probably been run off by bigger bulls. His entire objective is to find a cow or two and run off with her until he gets his way.

A neat trick to force a herd bull into showing himself is to rush him, screaming intensely and angrily on your bugle call as you go. Be sure the wind is in your favor and that you don't intrude so closely that he or his cows can see you. What you want to do is infuriate the old master by entering his territory. Some bulls will be pushed only so far, and then they'll come on the fight.

Basic elk calls include bull bugles (top row), cow calls (middle row), and diaphragm mouth calls (bottom row) with which you can make both bull and cow sounds.

Cow Calling

But better yet is using the cow call. Fifteen years ago, the cow call was unknown. Introduced to the hunting world by a veteran Montana elk hunter, the call nicely imitates the chirp made by a cow elk. Consider the enormous array of possibilities here. Instead of sounding like a challenging bull, you can utter sweet nothings and duplicate the exact vocalization of a cow. Many herd bulls will leave their cows to check out the new lady on the block, who is you, waiting with bow or firearm.

It's important to understand this: Unlike bulls that bugle during the breeding season, cows vocalize every day of the year. They communicate with each other and their calves while feeding and traveling, but almost never when they're bedded. This being the case, the cow call can be used effectively any time elk season is on. Since elk are extremely gregarious and band together in herds, the cow call is a tremendous tool in locating and enticing elk to your location.

Cows are very vocal all year long, and bulls know the females' talk. So try a cow call. A bull is more likely to come looking for some sweet-talking cow and a little potential breeding action, rather than a knock-down, drag-out fight with an ornery, challenging bull.

Bowhunting for Elk

Practically all bowhunters pursue elk during the rut, when the quarry can be called in with bull and cow calls. You must be mobile and in good physical condition, able to go where the elk are.

Compound bows are by far the most popular among hunters, with fewer using recurves, and far fewer using longbows. The compound has a system of pulleys, cams and strings, all of which work in harmony to produce a "let-off" which allows the shooter to draw back the string and hold it for a long period of time. This is important; you may have to wait, at full draw, for a bull to step out "just so" for you.

Elk hunters typically use bows with draw weights of 60 to 65 pounds or more. Arrows were once made of wood and fiberglass, but the modern versions are usually constructed of carbon and aluminum. Arrows must be matched to the bow and the draw length of the shooter. Broadheads vary widely, but basically include cutting edge and expandable heads. The most common have two, three or more blades, and some blades are detachable razor inserts. Elk hunters all have their preferences; practically all the popular broadheads will work on elk, though the 125 grain is preferred by many elk hunters.

The key, of course, is making an accurate shot. Most hunters these days use bowsights of some sort, but equally important is to be able to precisely judge distances, especially since elk hunters are normally on the ground and the target may appear instantly at any location.

Bowhunter checking out an elk wallow. Patient waiting, downwind, might get you a shot.

Using Calls

So how do you learn to use bull and cow calls? Attempting to describe these sounds by the written word is a worthless endeavor; your best bet is to rent or buy one of the many videos or cassettes on the subject and listen to and watch the instructors.

Remember a basic rule that many people don't: Bugle calls are largely a waste of time unless you're hunting during the breeding season, which is generally the month of September and into early October. The dates can vary a bit according to the region, elevation and latitude. This presents an interesting dilemma to firearms hunters. With a couple exceptions, most general elk rifle seasons begin in mid-October or later, purposely avoiding the rut. In some states you can hunt with a rifle during the rut in selected wilderness areas (requiring some formidable logistical efforts to gain access) and in some limited-entry units (requiring a lottery draw to obtain a tag).

Most bugling season hunts are bowhunting affairs (left), and every elk state has archery opportunities of this type. Rare indeed is the rifle bugling season hunt (right), but they can be had. These hunts are limited entry only.

If you're a bowhunter, however, you can hunt every major elk state during the rut, and in some cases, muzzleloader hunters may also hunt during the breeding season.

TRANSITION SEASON

Let's continue with our elk behavior discussion. Once the breeding season is over, bulls slowly leave their cows and head into seclusion, because this is the time of the general firearms season when the woods are suddenly swarming with hunters. All elk go on full alert, diving into the worst of the worst escape cover. This is what I refer to as the *transition* season, the toughest time to hunt.

Serious snows have not yet forced elk into lower elevations, and vocalization among bulls is over. What you have is an amazing, silent 700-pound animal who uses every bit of his incredible terrain to slip and sneak through awful cover. He can hide from you as easily as if he were a mouse. Therein lies the chief reason that so few of us tie a tag to an elk each year.

Author Jim Zumbo and a good bull elk taken during the transition season. Note the thick cover.

Understanding Elk

The Rocky Mountain elk is the primary subspecies of elk in North America, and the one you probably hunt or will get a chance to pursue.

Simply put, an elk is handsome, especially a mature bull with his tan coat, long and dark hair on the head and neck, and that sweep of huge, ivory-tipped antlers that may stretch well over half the length of his 7- to 8-foot-long body. A good bull will weigh anywhere from 500 to 750 pounds on the hoof. A cow is lovely too, and fully grown she'll push the scales to the 350- to 450-pound range. Her calf might weigh 25 to 35 pounds when it hits the ground.

Elk are tough to hunt, period. As I've said, the country is big

A cow watches as a big bull bugles, announcing dominance over and ownership of his harem.

and hard to get at. But once you're there, you have the elk's finely honed senses of smell and hearing to contend with, along with eyes that were made for spotting a predator's—your—movements. Ignore the wind, wear scratchy clothing and move too much or too quickly (or fidget around a lot as you wait) and you'll save an elk's life on your hunt.

An elk's year typically sees cows and bulls forming their own separate summer groups

as they disperse into the highlands after a long winter. There the cows drop their calves and raise them in lush alpine meadows where the feed is good; all the animals put on fat. In late summer, the bulls shed the velvet from their antlers and disperse for the rut, with the biggest and dominant bulls gathering harems of cows to breed. Most elk herds migrate when the big snows hit, heading to winter range where feed is available either because of less snow or because winds blow the snow from the forage.

Bull or cow, elk will be some of the finest big game eating you'll ever experience, and that's largely because they are grazers like the beef cattle we are so used to eating. Elk graze in the summer and fall, and then switch from grasses to browse such as willow, aspen, polar, dogwood, even sage and bitterbrush, in winter.

Transition season is tough hunting, but often "it's all we got!" Use a topo map to find inaccessible hellholes away from the crowds, then gather up the gumption to go there and hunt. *If you want an elk now, it's the only way.*

Hunting the Transition

So how do you locate a bull "jungled" up in a horrid blowdown that almost defies human travel? If you're serious, and your mental attitude is positive, you get out of the pickup truck or ATV and penetrate the mountains and, using your compass or GPS, strike out for the hinterlands. Be in the woods long before shooting light in the morning, and glass the meadows and openings that elk feed in during the night. Likewise, stay in the woods until the last minute of shooting light, since elk often hesitate to wander into openings during full daylight, especially if hunter pressure is heavy.

Remember this bit of advice: Elk must eat, regardless of the army of hunters in the woods. The big animals commonly feed in meadows and clearings because that's where grass grows best. Elk like grass, so that's where you'll find them. But, and I'm being repetitive here, be absolutely aware that pressured elk aren't going to be feeding in clearings during shooting hours where hunters are about. You can take that to the bank. The few elk

that do, usually on opening morning, are either shot or sufficiently spooked not to do it again.

Therefore, do not—let me repeat—do not waste your time watching a grassy meadow during the day as thousands of hunters do each year, unless you're into meditating, yoga or something besides elk hunting. You will see zero elk, because they'll be deep in the timber, and will not appear in the meadow until the day yields to night, or night itself has fully blanketed the mountain.

Don't expect transition-season elk to be out feeding in open meadows during daylight. They will retreat to deep timber before day breaks and will only come out again when night has settled.

There are exceptions to the notion that elk don't show themselves in meadows during shooting hours. I'm referring to clearings tucked away from roads, in pockets or basins where few hunters travel. By serious scouting, you can find these little jewels in the woods and watch them early in the morning and late in the afternoon.

Get Away from the Truck or ATV, Hunt Hard

If you're physically incapable of hiking into the higher reaches of the mountains, hunt smart and have your pals drop you off on a road atop a ridge, and slowly spend the rest of the day working your way down to a lower road where you can be picked up at night.

But be aware that the closer you stay to the wheel of your pickup, the less chance you'll ever have of seeing a living, breathing elk. The choice is up to you.

On public land where access is good, you can count on plenty of other hunters. Let them work for you by moving elk around during the day. Find a spot in the timber near trails and sit there. Don't go to camp for lunch or a midday nap. Bring lunch with you and doze in the woods if you're whipped. You *should* be whipped if you're hunting elk correctly. Always keep yourself in a position where elk may show, even during the heat of the day when you assume nothing should or would be moving.

MIGRATION SEASON

With the breeding and transition seasons over, elk become victims of the weather during the time known as the migration season. This period is totally dependent on heavy snow blanketing the high elevations, causing a major exodus among animals. Unable to feed in several feet of snow, elk move to lower elevations where they seek adequate forage on traditional winter ranges.

This can be a time of great joy or great consternation among hunters, depending on whether mother nature cooperates or not. During some years, snow doesn't fall until the hunting season is over. All migration-season hunting efforts are in vain when snow fails to come, because the elk are absent from the lower elevations, and absent elk means no elk to shoot and tag.

The solution is either to hunt in regions where there are year-round resident elk that aren't impacted by migration requirements, or to send some heavy-duty prayers aloft, asking for snowfall. It's important to remember that many states don't stretch their elk seasons late into the fall, just as they don't allow firearms hunting during the breeding season. Elk are simply very vulnerable during these two periods.

Above: Migration-season hunting is good hunting, but it can be rough and tough, and it is often done in bone-chilling cold. The rewards are worth it though. Left: Good snowfall becomes your friend when hunting migration-season elk, pushing them out of the high country where you can get at them.

It's hard work just planning an elk hunt, but all the effort pays off once you're in magnificent elk country like this.

PLANNING THE HUNT

Once you've established which of the three seasons you want to hunt, you must then make some important decisions. You must choose a state, and determine whether you want to hunt on your own or with an outfitter.

Select a State

Selecting a state is not an easy task. With one exception—Colorado—all the major elk states require nonresidents to obtain a tag either in a lottery draw, or on a first-come, first-served quota basis. In Colorado, you can still buy a general tag across the counter for most hunt units, but be aware that you *must* produce a hunter safety card if you were born after 1949.

This brings up another profound point. All states were not created equal. Be sure you understand the precise rules related to applying for an elk tag. Read the applications thoroughly—if in doubt, call the state wildlife agency (see *Resources,* page 203) and ask for clarification on points you have questions on. Nowadays you can look up rules and regulations on the Internet too. Unfortunately, the mere act of getting an elk tag is really not "mere." It can be a terribly frustrating effort.

You might not receive a limited-entry tag every year, but keep applying and sooner or later you'll draw out for the hunt of a lifetime. Here's author Jim Zumbo with a good bull from a limited-entry zone.

One of the great allures of elk hunting: the fine public-land opportunities available. It just feels good to get out, see all that country and know you can roam at will.

Limited-Entry Tags

Give yourself better odds of having a successful hunt by applying for a limited-entry tag. This is a tag that's good only for a specific unit that offers a quota of tags to residents and nonresidents alike. Because of the restricted number of hunters, the quality of elk is far better than in a general-hunt unit, as are the odds of taking a bull.

Because these limited-entry tags are tough to obtain, many states now offer bonus or preference points that will allow you to increase your odds in the drawing state. In fact, if you build enough preference points, you're guaranteed a tag someday, but the number of minimum points you need depends on the unit. Of course, units with plenty of big bulls are the toughest to draw. Call the state's wildlife agency to obtain data on applications made for each unit, preference points you might need, and other information.

I'm sold on the process. A couple years ago I drew a limited-entry tag for a unit in Colorado. I hunted public land, camped free and saw 11 bulls before I shot a 6-pointer that dropped a short distance from the road. To top it off, I saw only a handful of hunters. Remember, I took a 6-point bull on public land and wasn't involved in the chaos of a typical public-land hunt that occurs when you hunt with a general tag. I've been accumulating preference points ever since that hunt,

and now I have enough to once again draw that unit. Points work differently in the various states, so write or call for rules or check the Internet.

Do It Yourself?

Obviously, hunting elk on your own requires an enormous amount of planning.

A zillion questions must be answered, such as precisely where you will hunt, where you'll camp, what gear you'll need and myriad other details.

Should you plan an elk hunt on your own with a couple buddies? The good news is that every elk state has tens of millions of acres of public land inhabited by elk. These are chiefly lands administered by the U.S. Forest Service and the U.S. Bureau of Land Management. National forests commonly have plenty of roads providing good access, with numerous campgrounds.

Because it's off-season for tourists, many campgrounds are available at no charge, and in many forests you can camp practically anywhere along the road. The same is true of the BLM, but much BLM land is in lower elevations where elk do not exist. Obviously, check out the status of elk before hunting low country. If you aren't into camping, you can often stay in a motel and drive to the hunting area every morning, but be aware that motels in small towns are often booked well in advance of hunting season.

Muzzleloader Hunting for Elk

*I*t's important to be familiar with rules of the state you hunt before heading out with a muzzleloader, since some states have restrictions on firearms and accessories. Several states have muzzleloader-only seasons, enabling hunters to pursue elk during the rut.

No other shooting industry has had as much recent technological advancement as muzzleloading. In fact, the term "blackpowder" is now obsolete because blackpowder has largely been replaced by Pyrodex, a blackpowder substitute.

Another major change is the advent of the in-line rifle designed by William Knight in 1985. Basically, there are several types of muzzleloaders—the flintlock that depends on loose powder to fire externally, then sending a spark to the main charge behind the projectile; the standard percussion rifle that is fired by ignition of a cap; and the in-line that operates like the standard percussion, but all firing components are in a straight line.

Projectiles vary enormously, from round balls to conical bullets to sabots. The sabot is simply a factory bullet inserted into a plastic cup. They range in size from 180 grains to 325 grains. Most elk hunters like the heavier sabots fired by at least 100 grains of powder. Both .50 and .54 caliber guns are used by elk hunters, with the .50 caliber typically the most popular in elk camp.

Experienced hunters know that each gun has a "sweet" load—one that it performs best with. It's a good idea to experiment extensively to see what works best for you.

A muzzleloader of at least .50 caliber packs plenty of punch for an elk. Use a heavy saboted bullet (at least 250 grains but more likely 300) and 100 grains or more of Pyrodex to put a bull down for keeps. Work up a load that shoots well in your gun.

Hire an Outfitter?

Because of the enormous amount of knowledge, gear and physical effort required, some hunters opt to hunt with an outfitter. There are a few important things to remember here.

First and foremost, do not assume that an outfitter will guarantee you an elk. If he does, and if he's sincere, you'll be hunting inside a pen. Game farm elk are stupid and are not *hunted* but merely shot. You wouldn't and shouldn't be proud of that kind of elk.

All an outfitter can offer you regarding a truly wild elk hunt is this: an honest hunt where he'll make every effort to get you within shooting range of an elk. Most outfitted camps offer a 50 percent chance of scoring; some run higher, some lower. Before booking, check an outfitter's references by calling them, and check out other hunters who were in camp but were not on the referral list. You can get their phone numbers by referred clients who often exchange business cards during the hunt.

Remember to try to talk to unsuccessful hunters as well, to get a different perspective on the hunt, and how hard the outfitter worked.

Find out how many hunting days you'll have, how much hiking or horseback riding is required, camp accommodations, the quality of elk available, and other details. The more you can learn before the hunt the better. Outfitted hunts generally range from $2,500 to $4,500 for a five-to seven-day hunt. Some can be much higher, but if they're lower, get a bit suspicious and do some thorough preliminary checking.

Outfitters: Pluses & Minuses

The advantages of hunting with an outfitter are numerous. Basically, he'll transport you to the backcountry or allow you to hunt private land that he's leased. In either case, his objective is to get you away from crowds of other hunters, taking you to where the elk hunting is a quality experience. He'll also determine the hunting strategies to be used, provide for your sleeping and eating needs, and essentially tend to your comforts. And finally, he'll probably take care of the monumental task of dressing, quartering and getting your elk

One advantage of using an outfitter: He or she can get you into great elk country and back out again, and tote your meat and trophy out as well. These pluses (work saved) can outweigh the minuses (lost independence) of using an outfitter.

out of the woods and to your vehicle or to a meat processor. This last item is a big deal, and may be worth the price of hiring an outfitter in itself; you'll know what I mean when you walk up on a 700-pound elk you just shot and say "Oh my ..."

The disadvantages of using an outfitter are the cost, and, because you need to follow a guide, a lost sense of independence. These two factors are important to some hunters, and unimportant to others.

A workable compromise is to hunt out of a drop camp, which is exactly what the name implies. An outfitter drops you off at a camp he's already set up, and leaves your party to fend for yourselves. He'll probably take you in by horse and check on you every couple days, bringing you and your gear and meat out at the end of the hunt. Unfortunately, some of the biggest ripoffs perpetrated by outfitters are drop camps. Because the profits are slim (most drop camps cost around $1,000 give or take a couple hundred), some shady outfitters will establish camps in places that are easy to access and have few, if any, elk.

Another motivation for the outfitter to establish marginal camps is to keep you away from his fully guided (and higher paying) clients in the more expensive camps. He doesn't want you interfering with those hunts, and he knows that you might learn the country at his expense and return as a competitor on your own later (if he's operating on public land). For all those reasons, check out a potential drop camp thoroughly.

The news on drop camps isn't all bad. There are some excellent ones available in prime elk country. Do your homework beforehand; that's the bottom line.

AFTER THE SHOT

The need to get your elk out of the woods may quite possibly be the toughest part of the hunt. If you've got an outfitter, get your picture taken and sit back; you might help a little though. If you're hunting on your own, shoot a roll of film because then the work begins.

Consider the task—once the animal is down you'll be faced with the prospect of transporting an animal that weighs anywhere from 400 pounds

Elk is down, hunters are happy. But a bull elk, any elk for that matter, is one big critter. Now the real work begins.

and up for a mature cow, to 700 pounds and up for a mature bull. Do not take this chore lightly. Too many hunters are ignorant of the problem until they've squeezed the trigger and realized they're a mile or more from the road, most of it uphill.

The best way to transport an elk is to shoot it where you can drive to it, and have five husky pals who will help you lift it onto the pickup. Unfortunately, that scenario is rare; your elk is apt to fall where it will need to be cut up into pieces in order to move it.

A horse is a superb means of transportation, but you'd better know more than a little about horses. Packing is a skill, as is horsemanship. Most hunters don't own horses, but there's often the option of hiring a packer to bring your elk out, or to rent horses and use them yourself. Remember that it takes two horses to pack one bull elk.

If a horse isn't available, you might need to carry the elk out in quarters or chunks of boned meat. Be sure you have a very sharp knife as well as a sharpener, and a lightweight saw. Have all the equipment you need in your backpack, such as meat sacks, rope, and plastic bags for the meat. Your pack frame is infinitely important, because it will carry the lashed meat on your back. Practice hauling heavy loads with your pack before the

A couple of horses are perfect for carrying out a downed elk. Packing and horsemanship are acquired skills—learn them beforehand or hunt with someone who already has this expertise.

hunt. Assume that a quarter from a mature bull will weigh between 85 and 100 pounds. If that's too much for you, then bone the meat into smaller chunks and make more frequent trips with lighter loads.

A wheeled carrier is an excellent means of moving meat. Rolling any payload on a wheel is far better than dragging or carrying it. You can buy a commercial model or make one yourself. Never attempt to drag an elk unless you have a

downhill route all the way, or you have an NFL squad to help. Unless you are very big and in better shape than a triathlete, you won't be dragging an elk uphill no matter what the grade. Even dragging it on the level might be out of the question.

If you have an ATV, be sure you're familiar with off-road rules, and use the machine in an ethical manner. That means stay on marked trails as much as possible (i.e., the only time you should be off the road is to get to the kill site), and don't disturb other hunters.

Packing out an elk by foot. This is just the antlers and cape ... be prepared for at least four more trips. Choose your elk hunting partners carefully—their attitude in getting work done could really come into play, as will yours.

Here's a rare sight—whole elk! Most harvested elk you see are in quarters by the time they reach camp or road. This photo gives you an idea of how huge a bull elk is.

A trophy elk. His mother is a trophy, as is his father and some 6-point bull off on another mountain. Zumbo's Rule is true—any elk is a good elk.

SOME FINAL ADVICE

Do you want a trophy elk, a really big boy sporting six massive, long points to the side? If so, you're looking for an old bull—one that's survived at least five hunting seasons. You won't likely find him in places where there's good public access during a general season. You'll need to seek him in the hinterlands where there are few hunters, or in a limited-entry unit where there are few hunters, or on private land where there are few hunters. Catch my drift? The fewer hunters the better. But if you're like me, a trophy is in the eye of the beholder. I'm a firm believer in the old saying—*any elk is a good elk*. Once you've spent a little time in the elk woods, you'll know exactly what I mean.

52

Elk Rifles & Optics

Perhaps the most common question I'm asked when I give elk hunting seminars is the caliber of rifle to use. I don't believe there's only one perfect elk rifle, as some folks do. Most rifles will work fine, just as a Ford or Jaguar will get you to the same destination, but one offers more class and will get you there faster.

Choose a rifle with sufficient energy to push a bullet with adequate velocity, as well as enough foot-pounds of energy. The latter is the most important, with a minimum of about 1,500 foot-pounds at point of impact. I believe a .270 is the lightest you should consider for elk, and I'd suggest a larger caliber if you are up for it. I shot my first 19 bulls with a .30-06, and currently I've been

Although you can go as light as .270 caliber for an elk gun, a better [choice] would be something bigger. The .30-06 is plenty of gun, as are the 7[mm] .300 and .338 mags if you can take the recoil. Use a bolt action, per[haps]

seeing a lot of a 7mm Rem. Mag. The .300 and .338 mags are ideal choices if you can take the rough treatment of the hefty recoil. An elk is a big animal with bones much larger than those of deer. Keep that in mind. You may also expect shots out to 300 yards in elk country. Beyond that range, accuracy gets iffy.

My favorite .30-06 bullet is a 165-grain Federal Trophy Bonded Bear Claw. For those who want a heavier projectile, the 180-grain is also an effective elk load. The 140-grain Fail-Safe Supreme made by Winchester works well in the .270, and is a favorite of many elk hunters.

I've been a fan of a bolt action ever since I began reading Jack O'Connor when I was a kid. As with everything else, different actions appeal to different people. My only objection would be against the semiauto, which is likely to jam at an inopportune time, especially since elk hunting offers snow, sleet, ice and pesky branches and forest debris swishing against and into the action. I don't want any more problems than I already have when I'm elk hunting. I've seen enough semiautos jam that I'm wary of them, and I don't mind telling you so.

Optics are a must. A dependable scope that is lightweight, offers clear resolution and doesn't fog is mandatory. Though the 3X9 scope is very popular, I've gotten along with a straight four power for most of my adult life. Binoculars should likewise be of a quality brand, and they should be lightweight, easily focused and waterproof.

Elk are big and truly tough animals. You need to know your rifle and shoot it well to have any chance at success.

MULE DEER: A CRASH COURSE FOR BIG BUCKS

BY JIM VAN NORMAN

His magnificent antlers create a spectacle that draws your breath away. He is a package of intelligence—via magical disappearances in vast, wide-open terrain as well as mountain strongholds—and is equal to his white-tailed cousins in the "smarts" department. His sleek, gray, stocky beauty—accented by whites and blacks—is unique among North American big game. He soars with four-legged hops, unlike any other deer species, ensuring a fast and ground-consuming escape.

What are we talking about? You guessed it—BIG mule deer bucks—magicians in their habitat and never easy to locate let alone hunt and harvest. If you hope to take a good mule deer buck, one of the magical creatures of mystery and beauty, here's what you'll have to do.

MULE DEER SURVIVAL STRATEGIES

Mostly because of increased hunting pressure, today's mature mule deer bucks have developed personalities that cause them to lead very cautious lives—sometimes to the point of becoming totally nocturnal. As this becomes more and more common, a hunter's quest for a mule deer buck of a lifetime will

A buck mule deer at full alert—eyes, ears and nose. Extreme senses and a sneaky personality let many mule deer bucks— more than you think—grow old and gray.

become increasingly more difficult. But there are some fundamentals that will always remain the same no matter what happens with muley bucks, short of them developing any new technology; what they already have is awesome.

Extreme Senses

Mule deer possess extreme senses. I often use the term "extreme" when writing about a mule deer's senses, because there is no better way to describe them: abnormally acute, even keen beyond belief at times.

I liken a mule deer's ability to hear as sonar and his ability to see as radar. Bucks and does seem to pick up the slightest sounds at great distances, and their ability to pick up the slightest movement is uncanny. Their peripheral vision is also extraordinary. In addition, a mule deer has one of the finest noses on any critter.

So to be an effective big buck mule deer hunter, you'll have to defeat each of these senses. Let me

put it to you this way ... when I hunt a big buck's territory, I pretend that the big buck I'm after is a ruthless sniper dug in somewhere in the countryside looking for *me*. It's imperative that I find him first—before he gets a bead on me—or I'm dead (i.e., that opportunity is gone).

A buck can bust you with his eyes, and also effectively take you out of the equation with his ears and nose. To ignore any one of his senses or underestimate a big mule deer's sensory abilities is a grave mistake that will cost you dearly. By conducting yourself as if a sniper were looking for you, you will consistently be more effective on these mule deer monarchs. (The details on how to sneak about mule deer country and find them before they find you appear later in this chapter.)

Sneaky Personality

In general, mule deer prefer to leave an imminently dangerous area quietly, and move far ahead of the potential problem, rather than wait

Never skyline yourself while mule deer hunting. A buck's eyes will pick you up every time; he'll sneak out the back door (or stay right where he is) and you'll never know he was there.

Here's a common hunter evasion tactic that big buck mule deer use: Get up and calmly walk away at the first hint of danger.

and see what's going to happen. So a bigger, smarter buck will generally place himself in a position that affords him the opportunity to see great distances and smell or hear what he can't see. Or bucks put themselves in the deepest, thickest cover available where they become invisible to all predators, man or beast. When surprised, a buck will lay his ears back and hide motionless, letting you walk by within mere feet. Bucks are also known for waiting until you are desperately close and then flushing like a pheasant at your feet, leaving you rattled and without a shot.

Even though they possess many tricks, big mule deer bucks prefer to calmly sneak out far ahead, unnoticed and before the danger can get close. This is an important point to remember while honing your skills as a top-notch mule deer hunter.

Mule deer bucks, especially the bigger, more mature deer, are large critters compared to most of their white-tailed cousins. Some large bucks can weigh upwards of 300 pounds on the hoof. It is a wonder to many inexperienced mule deer hunters how a deer this big can hide so well, even in such open terrain as that where I live and do much of my mule deer hunting. Keep in mind I am referring to the big bucks that have seen quite a few hunting seasons come and go. Younger bucks and some does are generally readily visible and unconcerned, hence the reputation mule deer have for being easy to hunt.

Wherever you find them, mule deer bucks are not easy to spot. Look at the color on this buck—just like the rocks! This guy's up and moving, but if he were bedded right now, spotting him would not be easy.

But the caliber of bucks I am giving you tactics for here are a different breed than the average mule deer. Even though they are of considerable size they use their coloration to the max. Nature has created the mule deer's colors to perfectly match the habitat in which they hang out. For example, deer in the wide-open sagebrush country tend to be more deep gray and have lighter colored antlers than their neighbors up in the timber. The deer in the timber possess more browns throughout their coats, and their antlers are generally darker. I've seen this transition within only a few miles between wide-open country and tree-covered hills. It's amazing how nature helps deer adapt "camo" to match the habitat they live in.

Understanding Mule Deer

It's hard to say what is a better symbol of the great American West—the pronghorn, elk, bison or mule deer—but I'd put my vote in for the mule deer.

He inhabits deserts, plains, prairies, ranchlands, riverbottoms and breaks, foothills, mountainsides and mountain peaks … all the magnificent country the West has to offer. His handsome, double-forked antlers sweep wide and high, a reflection of the big country he calls home.

His blocky, gray body blends perfectly with his habitat, and the coat varies from desert to prairie to fir-studded mountain. A good buck on the prairies or in the mountains will easily hit 200 pounds; many bucks will hit 300 pounds if they get old enough. Does will weigh 150 to 160 pounds.

How do mule deer get old? Bucks and does alike do it with those huge, gray ears that gather in sound from every direction of the compass, and a nose that knows what's going on everywhere in the vicinity. Couple that with prying eyes and the calm but cautious personality I've discussed, and you're going to have to hunt smart to fool a mule deer.

Like other deer, a mule deer is a browser, and he needs a steady supply of shrubs and brush as forage. Sage is a key winter food. Where hay meadows, wheat fields and other agriculture exist, mule deer will readily hit the crops too.

One of the most amazing things you'll notice, upon seeing a mule deer that decides to move out, is his pogo-stick gait, called *stotting*. This hop-hop-hop locomotion allows him to get over obstacles quickly, change direction on a dime, and climb even the steepest slopes with ease; his ability to combine these movements lets him leave a ground-based predator far behind. A stotting mule deer is fun to watch, but if you do see one, chances are you've made a hunting blunder, and it's time to get busy and hunt up another deer.

Mule deer buck and does.

KEY EQUIPMENT: OPTICS

Now that you have a basic feel for the type of critter you are after, let's talk about the optics you will need to be an effective big buck mule deer hunter.

Binoculars

One of the most important pieces of equipment you'll need is a great pair of binoculars. Clarity and light-gathering capabilities are of utmost importance. There *is* a difference, so shop carefully. Windriver (Leupold), Steiner, Swarovski and Leica are good choices. I recommend 7X35s or 8X40s for carrying in the field. Depending on how you look at it, 10-power glasses are either too heavy to carry for long distances or so light you can't hold them still for several days' worth of glassing without major eyestrain. If you insist on the stronger power, make sure you carry a tripod and use it. Eyestrain can cause you to miss a big buck lying in a good spot for a stalk, or cause you to stop glassing (to rest your eyes) just when you should be bearing down hard to find that buck before nightfall.

You'll need good binoculars wherever mule deer bring you. On the prairie (left), you'll be glassing draws, gulleys, cutbanks, nooks, crannies and various other hiding spots, many of which are a long ways away. Your bare eyes won't do the job at all. Even in timbered country (above), good binoculars are a must for picking out mule deer "pieces and parts" in the cover, and across canyons or drainages.

I choose binoculars that have individual rotating eye pieces so I can adjust the binoculars to my eyes only. Then I mark the setting with a felt tip marker. Make sure the eye pieces have enough friction so that, once they are set, they will more than likely stay set. I always look at the settings quickly before I bring my glasses to my eyes, in case the settings have been inadvertently moved. There is nothing harder on your eyes than pulling your binoculars up and rolling a center focus ring back and forth until your view is focused. It might be okay if you only adjust your glasses a few times a day, but on a mule deer hunting trip you would be rolling that focus ring hundreds of times a day as you glass. You're in for major headaches and eyestrain deluxe if you don't heed this advice, and you won't see many mule deer if you're not using your optics a lot.

The point is: Get a pair of binoculars that, once pulled up to your eyes, are focused and ready to serve you. Note: If you already have a pair with center focus, give them to the kids and get a pair that will afford you hours and days of intense glassing without eyestrain or headaches.

Spotting Scope

A good spotting scope is a must for mule deer country. I choose to use a straight 20-power scope. Anything larger or variable also causes major eyestrain. I have a friend who lost his right eye because of major eyestrain, zooming between 12- and 60-power for three days straight on a Red Desert antelope hunt. On the last afternoon of his hunt he felt a "pop" in his eye and lost his vision in that eye forever. Plus, due to heat waves and air quality, there are very few times during a normal day when the conditions are right to use a magnification higher than 20-power effectively and for any length of time.

Consider a good 20-power spotting scope necessary gear. This bowhunter has located a muley buck a mile-and-a-half out. Only a spotting scope can give the hunter a good enough look to decide whether it's a buck he wants, and to plan the stalk's detailed route.

Bows for Mule Deer

Pick a bow with 50 to 80 pounds of draw weight. I shoot 65 pounds at everything from a moose to a mouse. The main thing here is to pick a bow and a draw weight you are comfortable shooting and can draw with very little strain. Almost all of today's modern compounds are fantastic shooters, but use a more traditional recurve or long bow if you wish. You will add to your challenge, but that's why you choose a bow as a weapon anyway.

I prefer fixed-blade broadheads, either of solid construction or with inserts. While guiding bowhunters, I've seen too much inconsistency in the way impact-type broadheads open up on game. It's a great concept if it would only work every time without fail, but that hasn't yet been my experience. If the manufacturers get the bugs worked out and achieve reliable, guaranteed blade opening, these will be great products.

Sight your bow in with pins from 10 to 40 yards. Any bow shot longer than 40 yards in the wide-open spaces is generally pretty risky.

Perri Van Norman, the author's wife, with a good buck. You don't need a ton of draw weight to shoot mule deer, you just need to know how to shoot. Use a fixed-blade broadhead for reliable performance.

You may disagree with me on this point, but many a time I've wondered why I spent the extra money on a variable 12 to 40- or 60-power spotting scope when the image is always clearer at 20 power. At 30, 40 and 60 power I generally have to get closer anyway to see for sure if the buck is one I want to go after—because of poor image quality at the higher powers. Suit yourself here, but if you are on a budget like most folks, stick to a good quality 20-power spotting scope and spend the extra cash on binoculars or snake bite medicine!

FINDING BIG BUCKS

Once you have a good pair of binoculars and a good spotting scope, the next question is where do I find big mule deer? I could go into a long and complicated description here but it's truly not necessary. There are only two places to find the biggest bucks your hunting area has to offer. One is in the roughest, toughest country your chosen area has to offer. The other place is simply in the shade.

Big, experienced bucks hide out where the country is the toughest. Once in a while early in the season, usually in bow season, you will see

Shade, shade, shade. Look in the shade. Bucks like to lie in the shade. That's where to look.

them down in reasonably easy country. But when fall draws near, these bucks are smart enough to head for the hills and canyons of hell, where they have survived the hunting seasons up until now.

Shade is generally where you find all mule deer bucks regardless of the country you've chosen to

Big buck mule deer love rough, rocky, lonely, forgotten places. Go there, and not to the pretty, classic-looking country you can get to (and out of) easily.

hunt. They feed in the shade, they bed in the shade and they hide in the shade. If you concentrate your glassing efforts on the shady spots, you'll find more big bucks than the average hunter.

Where do you find shade? Below trees, of course; look under single ones too. But also look behind a rock. Under the lip or edge of a gully. Under a cutbank. It doesn't take a lot of shade to make a mule deer happy; check out every little patch.

HUNTING UP A BIG BUCK

There are many critical parts to mule deer hunting, but there are really only four basic concepts that you must master to be consistently a top-notch mule deer hunter: scrolling, skirting, pieces and parts, and stalking. These are not hard concepts to learn, but it takes effort and discipline to put them to work.

Scrolling

As discussed earlier, it is imperative to see a big buck long before he sees, hears or smells you; that's the only way you'll ever have an opportunity to stalk him. The tried-and-tested concept you should master here is "scrolling."

Author Jim Van Norman peeking through the mass of antlers on one of the many great bucks he has taken. Take the time to "scroll" while you hunt and you too will shoot more mule deer, maybe one as good as this.

You probably know better than to skyline yourself on *any* horizon while moving about in a particular piece of hunting country. And if skylining becomes necessary, while moving from one drainage to the next, most diligent hunters know to crouch over and be only momentarily visible while skylining (taking advantage of all available cover). The idea of scrolling is to keep from being visible to all living things in the drainage you've chosen to hunt. Here's how to scroll:

As you come to the crest of ridge, hill, canyon, rise (any kind of elevation or terrain you want to see over), just as soon as you can see any portion of the country beyond the crest, stop and take a quick look with the naked eye, then begin glassing. Use the crest line of the terrain in front of you as your "underscore" line, the line hiding your body from view. Glass the landscape above the line thoroughly. Then move forward ever so slightly and begin the process of looking with the naked eye and then glassing once again. In effect, you are scrolling up the next piece of territory lying directly below the first. Accomplish this from your belly, knees or feet, whatever you feel is warranted for the situation. If you elect to stay on your feet, make certain you have a backdrop of some sort to prevent skylining. Always remember to move very slowly.

Here's what you want to see when scrolling—some antlers or ears, but not a deer looking back at you. This way you can back off and plan your approach.

Scrolling in action. Approach a rise inch by inch, peeking over the top and "scrolling" slivers of new country into view. You'll spot deer before they spot you.

By scrolling up small portions of country at a time, you'll soon begin to spot deer that are totally unaware of your presence before they spot you, because you are "peeking" over at them and not barging up in full view. This method also affords you the opportunity to then back off and stalk into position for a better look, if you see something you like. You'll also be in a position to carefully plan an effective stalk, or maybe even come back over for a shot.

If there are places that are out of your field of view as you scroll up a piece of country, and you think they may be hiding a big muley, back up below the horizon and move laterally 50 yards or so. Then start your scrolling process again from a different angle. Repeat this process as necessary to get a look into all the different pockets of cover. You'll be surprised at what you see from a different viewpoint.

Scrolling is the solution to finding mule deer long before they find you in any terrain. Just a little patience and extra effort provide great opportunities in the form of mule deer spotted before they spot you.

Skirting

The next concept is skirting. Skirting means to travel along a ridge laterally, just below the ridge line and out of sight of the "primary" side you want to hunt. Make certain the wind is blowing toward you and away from the primary hunting side. Scroll up into position for a look at the drainage you hope to find a buck in. Thoroughly glass narrow corridors 100 to 200 yards wide within your scope of view. If nothing is found, then back off below the horizon and move down the ridge 100 to 200 yards. If after scrolling again you determine there is nothing within view, back up below the crest (again out of sight) and proceed down the ridge another 100 to 200 yards.

Always take another look at the corridors previously glassed from your new location, as you'll now be looking at them from a different angle. This is very important because it is impossible to see down into all the breaks, pockets and

Equipment Notes

In addition to a sighted-in weapon that you can shoot well, other equipment necessary to be a good mule deer hunter includes a good pair of waterproof hiking boots with lots of support, layered clothing (so you can add and remove layers as your activity level and the weather change), and a good hat with ear flaps. You also need a good daypack with lunch and snacks, water, and necessary survival gear should you have some type of accident and have to spend the night in the great outdoors. Where truly big mule deer bucks hang out, the country is generally mean and the weather unforgiving. If you aren't prepared, there's a fair chance they'll only find your bone pile the following spring. So be prepared for anything when you come out West on a quest for big mule deer!

Skirting in action. The bowhunter (left) has been sneaking his way down the back side of a ridge, creeping up to peek over every now and again, looking for a buck to stalk. The rifle hunter (right) is doing the same; he might get his shot this way without a stalk, considering the rifle's range.

washouts in mule deer country from just one position. Repeat this sequence as you slowly work your way along. Note that there will always be country behind you that you are totally exposed to. Your main concern should only be the country you've determined "primary." It is a good idea however, to stop and glass the country you are exposed to once in a while, just in case there is a buck out in the open or watching you from a distance; it happens!

Skirting, scrolling and glassing corridors seems like a lot of work but can make the difference between getting the buck of a lifetime or "cussing" under your breath as you watch him clear the far ridge!

Pieces & Parts

The third concept paramount to success is what I call "pieces and parts." The difference between the average mule deer hunter and the successful big buck hunter is in the latter's ability to spot deer. My pieces and parts concept lays the groundwork for you to find that monster buck before he sees you.

Here's how. Now that you've skirted and scrolled into position, here's what to look for:

You'll seldom see a mule deer—especially a big buck like this—standing stark out in the open. Instead, you have to know what "pieces and parts" to look for.

When glassing, I seldom concern myself with looking for a whole deer at once. Instead, I concentrate my attention on images representing a few key parts of a mule deer. It's important to train your mind to alert your eyes when one of these key images is scanned, and immediately go back and look again for confirmation. As with all of these images, once a particular part is found, it is important to begin building the other parts of the deer—the pieces attached to the specific part you have discovered.

As mentioned, big mule deer bucks tend to select places to rest and bed that are, in most cases, well hidden or that at least take full advantage of the deer's natural camouflage. While in the field you will seldom have the opportunity to view a bedded buck from stem to stern. There will most likely be only a small portion of him sticking out of his hiding spot. There are as many as 16 images that I use to decode the presence of a mule deer when glassing. For the purpose of this chapter I will give you only the core images of this technique. (For further reference of other images I use, consult the NAHC's book *Mule Deer—Western Challenge*, or my book *Mule Deer, Hunting Today's Trophies*, available by calling 1-800-258-0929.)

The acronym FERAL lays the foundation of this concept:

F stands for face. White is a color your eyes will easily pick up with your optics in most any terrain. A mule buck's muzzle is fairly white in the summer and early fall, but then turns *extremely* white with a buck's winter coat of gray. If a mule deer is well hidden, sometimes the only thing to betray him is his stark white face. This element is one of the top three images to key on and should be kept toward the top of your list mentally.

E stands for ears. Mule deer ears are among their most prominent features and are some of the most common parts you'll see while glassing. Their candle flame shape stands out very well in any terrain. They may also appear as a broad leaf of some type, always deserving of another look, because few broadleaf plants exist in most mule deer country.

R represents rump. The mule deer's rump is very noticeable even at great distances if the light is just right. There are plenty of other stark, round white spots in any landscape though, so you must check them all out. Here is a tip for quickly deciding whether the image you've spotted is actually attached to a mule deer: Upon returning to scrutinize the white spot, you should see a black spot toward the bottom of the white. That black spot, common to most all mule deer, is the tip of the tail. The tip will resemble an artist's paintbrush—wide at the base of the bristles and tapered to a fine point. In addition to the black tip, watch that spot for a bit. Mule deer will wag their tails often while feeding or in a relaxed state, and this will quickly confirm your suspicions.

A means antler. This image should also be in the top three "pieces and parts" considerations. Not only is it one of the most prominent thoughts on our minds while scanning for big buck mule deer, but it's also a very common element or part to see first. The reason: Although mule deer bucks hide their bodies quite well, they don't seem to have a good feel for how far their antlers rise up above their heads. It is common to see a mule deer buck's antlers sticking out like a sore thumb even though his body is well hidden. To confirm what you are looking at, study the image for the typical branched configuration of mule deer antlers—two points on the upper beam and two on the lower beam. Concentrate on the main frame as outlined and always glass for just one antler. Looking for one antler makes the work simpler and where there's one, there's customarily another—right there handy!

These bucks (at left and below) in the shadows display some of the pieces and parts you'll be looking for. Notice the rumps that are brighter than the surroundings, as well as the faces, ears, and antler configurations.

L is for legs. Typical mule deer habitat is full of objects that stick up perpendicular to the ground, but few of these objects are tightly bunched with no branches. From great distances, legs will appear to be three or four light-colored toothpicks protruding from the ground. Sometimes all you can see are two sticks, one behind the other, possibly with an angle in both (the two hind legs). A mule deer's legs are very light in color compared to most other parts of its body. This is especially true of the inside of the legs. Key on such objects and scan back for another look. As with all these images, start building the other components of a deer, for confirmation.

By memorizing the core images with the acronym FERAL (Faces, Ears, Rump, Antlers and Legs) and a little practice, you'll start spotting those monster bucks that the "average" hunter would otherwise spook out of the county.

Putting on the Stalk

The last concept that makes or breaks a big buck mule deer hunter—and separates the men from the boys and the women from the girls—is stalking. Even though the other concepts are vitally important and no matter how good you are at them, if you can't think like a human predator and "make like a mountain lion" you're not going to shoot any big buck mule deer. The many facets of stalking could make an entire book, so I'll do my best to keep it short and clear here. Keep in mind, you will learn far more from mule deer themselves than from me, which means: stalk every chance you get.

When picking a piece of country to hunt, choose rough, cut-up country with canyons, draws, cutbanks, washouts and limited vegetation. Not only does this type of country present more good opportunities for good stalks, but big bucks generally prefer this type of terrain. Leave the beautiful classic-looking country to the does and young bucks. Plus, mule deer's senses are so acute, success-ful stalking in heavy vegetation is tough and sometimes impossible. The same goes for open rolling hills. At best, both are low-percentage endeavors.

On the other hand, rough, cut-up and seemingly barren country presents more opportunities to approach unnoticed. So if you are planning to stalk, especially if you are just getting started mule deer hunting, pick an area that will present the highest percentage of opportunities.

Clothing and boot selection can be very important in pulling off a great stalk. The quieter your clothes and footwear, the better. Wool is a great outer garment for stalking. Waterproof boots with soft rubbery soles and no traction bars are my choices for getting in close when the weather's bad. In early fall and other times when the weather is good, I'll slip off my boots and slip on a pair of thick wool socks to finish my stalk in. Tuck in your pants legs.

There are three main considerations to beginning a successful stalk: evaluating the stalking opportunity, evaluating the wind, and mentally mapping a stalking route that is easy to follow.

First light, a good buck out in front of you ... get out the optics and watch, watch, watch until he beds. Mark his location, evaluate the wind and then map out your stalking route before going after him.

Stalking tip for bowhunters: Get out of your big clunky boots for the final approach—about the last 200 yards—and slip on a pair of thick, gray wool socks or Safari Stalkers (left). You'll be amazed at how quietly you can get around when you can feel every twig, rock, pebble and other potential noise-maker. Tuck your pants legs in too, to avoid making "swishing" sounds against sage and other vegetation.

Evaluate the stalking opportunity. Given the deer's position, your position, the terrain and the available cover, what are your chances of getting where you need to be? Stalk only when you have a very good or excellent chance to succeed. Don't force an opportunity from a bad situation, especially if it's a great buck. If you are a serious hunter, lie and wait for the buck to move and then reevaluate your chances … because you'll get only one.

Evaluate the wind properly. Is the breeze steady in your face, coming cross-lots or quartering? Or is it light and variable, making a stalk iffy? Remember— you want the wind blowing from the deer to you, or at least carrying your scent away.

Based on the wind, what will be your stalking route? A "goofy" wind blows more stalks than any other factor. Evaluating wind properly is key to selecting the right stalking opportunity. Don't go on a stalk without understanding what the wind is doing. If it's wrong, wait or go find another deer. A muley will smell you and evacuate if you give him the slightest warning.

Keep testing the wind as you stalk, whether you have rifle or bow in hand. It is folly to try to stalk a mule deer—any mule deer, not just a big old buck—when you know your scent will be blowing to the animal.

Wait for the Right Shot

When rifle hunting or muzzleloading, make sure checkpoint number three (page 72) provides you a clear, responsible shot at the vitals. If the shot angle isn't right, wait for the situation to develop. If you can do it, sneak to a different position to get a better shot. If you like the range and you have the patience, your best bet is to stay put, get a steady rest lined up and wait.

When bowhunting, checkpoint number three is where you wait for an opportunity for a responsible shot. This position should not be closer than 20 yards or farther than 30 yards if you can help it, because the deer may move. Make certain this position has a bush, rock, tree or something directly behind you to break up your outline. There should also be something small in front to help cover you there. Then wait. And wait some more. Wait for the shot to develop.

This tactic can't be overemphasized. Many bowhunters make a mistake at this point that costs them dearly. The mistake is forcing the situation by making the buck do something—like move, stand up, look away or anything else designed to get a shot quickly.

Not smart! Wait for the opportunity, no matter how long it takes. That buck won't lie there all day. You want to wait for a calm deer out there in front of you.

Do not force the situation when you're in position and ready to shoot. Be patient and let the buck get up or otherwise move of his own accord. You'll have a shot at a relaxed target, and probably more time to shoot as well.

Map a stalking route. This is an essential element. Plan a route containing three solid checkpoints that you can easily recognize as you close in on the deer. These landmarks should be prominent and reasonably uncommon so they are not easily confused when you're out in the stalk arena. It's always surprising how different the country looks when you start sneaking through it, as opposed to the view from where you glassed! It's also very frustrating when you get to where you thought the deer was, but blow him out because you ended up in the wrong place. Checkpoints along your stalking route are critical.

The first checkpoint should be a place where you can confirm you are on the right track after leaving your spotting location. Checkpoint two is the halfway point. Checkpoint three is the place where you will attempt a shot. (In bowhunting, this is the place where you wait for a shot to develop.)

Although the actual location of the deer is important and deserves a strong mental note, don't get in the habit of sneaking to the deer. Instead, concentrate on getting to the place from where you will attempt the shot. This technique will help curb your urge to check the deer's status.

One of the most common reasons that so many stalks are blown (besides an errant wind carrying your scent to the deer) is a hunter's misguided need to "sneak a peek" and continually check the status of the deer. My rule of thumb is: Never take another look at the deer you are stalking after the second checkpoint—until you arrive at checkpoint three. You know the deer's location as it relates to checkpoint number three, so concentrate on your foot placement and staying out of sight. Don't get busted three-quarters of the way (or more!) through your stalk.

Use the terrain as much as possible to totally cover your movements. Don't count on trees or bushes for cover as you approach. A mule's ability to catch the slightest movement, even if it is partially obscured, is unbelievable. Stay in the shade as much as possible while stalking: camouflage patterns and movement are much harder for deer to pick up in the shadows. Wear good camouflage in bow season and cover your face too.

Remember to use your binoculars as you stalk along. I use my binoculars for the distance work

Plan your stalking route well, even to the point of using your binoculars to identify specific "checkpoints" that will guide you step-by-step on your approach.

A swirling wind. Little clinks or clacks or clutters or other noises. Giving in and sneaking a look at the animal and blowing your cover. Lots of things can ruin your stalk, but one factor you may not think about is other deer—little bucks (left) and does (below) you didn't bother to locate before setting out after a big old buck. Once they go snorting and bounding off, you're done for.

of course, but I also use them right down to ranges as close as twenty feet. It is important to continually check along your route for other deer, deer you didn't see originally that could potentially blow your stalk. It's amazing how much more detail you can pick out, even at close range, with binoculars. It's also amazing how mad you can get when you stumble upon another deer that catches you in the act and blows your cover.

Stalking is a talent that you will more fully develop with time and many a failed stalk. But these basic stalking fundamentals will help you

eliminate years of experience (blown stalks) and become a more successful stalker in a shorter period of time.

A Special Critter Indeed

It only takes one trip to muley country to have big buck mule deer get into your system and never let you rest. Just one glimpse of a big mule deer topping the skyline will keep you dreaming until you find yourself back in big buck country, year after year. If you will concentrate on the hunting skills presented here you will find and take more big mule deer than most hunters ever see! Best wishes for good health and many successful mule deer seasons.

Mule Deer Rifles

My selections for best mule deer calibers, after years of guiding hunters and hunting for myself, are the .270, 7mm and .25-06. During my first 10 years of mule deer hunting, I used an old Winchester lever-action .30-30 saddle gun, and I took many a big mule deer with it. But my success was predicated more on stalking ability than ballistics: I got good and close to those bucks before I shot!

There are lots of different calibers that will kill a mule deer buck based on your ability as a hunter, but for maximum effectiveness on killing a big buck, flat shooting at long range, and minimum flinching on the part of the hunter, the calibers mentioned above are my choices. The venerable .30-06 works well too.

Consider 100 grains the minimum bullet weight you'll want to use for mule deer, and that's even a little light. 130 grains is more like it. Plenty of hunters use a 130-grain bullet in a .270 Winchester. It's a good, fast combo. You'll find most of the .30-06 and 7mm people shooting 140- to 180-grain bullets; 150- and 165-grain projectiles work well too, because they're big enough to hit hard and even buck the crosswinds a bit, yet lean enough to travel fast.

Action? Use a bolt: tough and reliable in the rainy, snowy, wet, dry, dusty, hot and cold West.

Scope selection is always a dilemma. All I can say in regard to this subject is to buy a scope of good quality with great clarity and light-gathering capabilities. It should be of solid tube construction to help eliminate the possibility of fogging. The tube length, between scope rings, should be long enough to accommodate eye relief suitable for the length of your rifle stock and your "build."

Variable scopes are fine if you know how to use them. I can't tell you how many times people have come to hunt with me and brought their 3 to 9 variable scopes, then walk around hunting with the scope cranked to 9 power. Invariably, a big buck jumps up right in front of us and the hunter can't find him in the scope to save his life! The only life he saves is the buck's. I always instruct my hunters to adjust their variable scopes to 3 or 4 power while hunting and then crank it up, if need be, for the shot. If budget is a factor, a straight 4-power scope is plenty adequate on any rifle, especially a muzzleloader, where most shots are normally less than 150 yards.

Sight your centerfire rifles in 2 inches high at 100 yards. That should cover most applications in the West, allowing you to hold "right on" out to 250 to 275 yards. Sight in your muzzleloader for 100 yards, then stick to that limit unless you're awfully handy at longer ranges.

Sight in your centerfire rifle to hit only about 2 inches high at 100 yards. You'll be able to hold right on out to 250-275 or so yards, and that's plenty of range in most mule deer hunting situations.

Chapter 5

Blacktails: Hunting the Pacific Ghost

By Bob Robb

Blacktails are often called the "Pacific Ghost," and with good reason. With few exceptions (Alaska's lightly-hunted Sitka blacktails and low-pressure Lower-48 private-land Columbia blacktails) these secretive deer spend their lives ghosting invisibly through the old-growth timber and coastal rain forest jungles from central California north to Alaska. A mule deer subspecies, blacktails live more like whitetails. They often have a relatively small home range, and the bigger bucks rarely expose themselves outside their thick-cover homes except, like whitetails, during the rut.

A blacktail buck in the thick stuff. You'll have to go into his turf and still-hunt super slowly, or else wait him out on a good stand.

How to Hunt

Blacktail hunting techniques vary greatly, depending on the area being hunted and time of year. Versatility is the key to all-season success.

Still-Hunting & Stand-Hunting

Still-hunting is popular with forest blacktail hunters who have incredible patience and who move

Waiting on stand for a blacktail is a lot like being in the whitetail woods—thick cover, maybe with agricultural crops nearby.

like overweight snails. That's because the country is so thick that the glassing techniques popular with open-country mule deer hunters are ineffective, and because the ever-present rainy weather that dominates the Pacific northwest can quiet the woods to a church-like stillness.

Sneaking along a deer trail that winds through chest-high ferns, thick berry tangles and ancient trees, stopping to look for a minute or two between steps, is as exciting as any hunting I've ever done. Blacktails are famous for letting you walk right past them. I once shot—at 10 steps—a dandy 3X3 in his bed; he had made the mistake of leaving one antler tip for me to see above the blackberries. Several times I've unknowingly walked right by bucks, confident I had searched the area completely yet found nothing, only to have them explode out behind me after I'd passed their beds.

Like all deer, blacktails love crops, and hunting the edges of agricultural areas can be a great way to fill your tag. Whether it be barley, wheat, alfalfa, apples, pears, even nuts ... if the fields border thickly-covered mountains you can bet there are deer nearby. Taking a stand along a field edge is a great way to intercept thieving bucks.

Hunt When It's Wet

Unlike many other forms of deer hunting, serious blacktail hunters drop everything and head for the woods when it's misting, raining, foggy or a combination thereof. The deer just seem to move better when it's wet outside. I shot my all-time best buck when, after a week of unseasonably hot, dry late-November weather, Medford, Oregon guide Doug Gattis and I woke on the next-to-last day of my hunt to a falling barometer, drizzling fog and a forecast of rain.

Early that morning we peeked around a corner and my heart almost stopped. A doe was placidly feeding while being tended by two bucks, one a very large 3X3 that would have been a "shooter" on any other day. His saving grace was the other buck, a perfect 4X4 that took my breath away. At only 60 yards, it was easy to settle the bead of my muzzleloader behind the front shoulder and squeeze the trigger. The buck's tall, heavy, perfectly symmetrical 4X4 antlers later officially scored 154⅛ points, which would place it at No. 58 in the all-time Boone and Crockett record book.

Author Bob Robb with a magnificent Oregon buck shot, of course, in the wet.

Never let rain or drizzle keep you out of the blacktail woods; that's when the hunting gets good!

Understanding Blacktails

Columbia blacktail buck.

There are two subspecies of blacktails: the more primitive Sitka blacktail (*Odocoileus hemionus sitkensis*) of the Alaska and British Columbia coast, and the more common Columbia blacktail (*Odocoileus hemionus columbianus*) found from central California north through coastal British Columbia. Columbia blacktails can and do readily interbreed with mule deer wherever their ranges overlap, creating several different hybrid mule deer subspecies.

Columbia blacktails live more like whitetails than mule deer, a function both of the thick cover they prefer and their extremely nocturnal nature. One study by the Oregon Department of Fish and Wildlife shows just how nocturnal mature blacktail bucks are. In this pre-rut study, special cameras were placed on six fall migration trails vacating the high Cascade Range en route to the deers' low-elevation winter range. The cameras were triggered by an infrared beam of light when an animal walked past, as well as registering the date and time the picture

was taken. The results were eye-opening. Of the 606 deer photographed (300 more "additional" events were recorded but not photographed), 87 percent of the bucks traveled at night, while 56 percent of the does and fawns traveled after dark. In addition, 42 percent of the bucks photographed were 4X4s or better.

Sitka blacktails like thick cover too, but because hunting pressure is relatively light, they generally don't take to the thick stuff as readily as their cousins do. In areas of thick timber, like Southeast Alaska and coastal British Columbia, they must often be rooted out of the old-growth forest, much like rooting out whitetails.

Blacktails have the same bifurcated antler configuration as their close cousins, the mule deer. For record-book purposes, they are scored exactly the same, they're just smaller. The classic

North American Hunter *editor Gregg Gutschow with a Sitka blacktail.*

Look at the tail on this doe. It's obvious where the blacktail gets its name!

trophy-class Columbia blacktail has heavy bases and beams, four points per side measuring at least 4 to 5 inches in length, noticeable eye guards, and an inside antler spread at least ear-wide. A whopper Sitka buck will have the same antler configuration, though the points will be much shorter. It should be noted that many large blacktail bucks of both sub-species often only have three points on one or both sides, with or without one or both eye guards—antlers that look more like classic whitetail horns than mule deer antlers. While they won't score high enough to make the record book, heavy-horned bucks of this type are trophy-class bucks nonetheless.

Mature Columbia blacktail bucks will weigh somewhere between 175 and 200 pounds on the hoof. Mature Sitka bucks can weigh as much, but because they have shorter legs and blockier bodies, they often appear to weigh less than they actually do.

Acorns and mushrooms are staples of the blacktail's diet, but these deer also love agricultural crops when they're available.

WHERE TO HUNT

To understand blacktail hunting, it's best to study the habitat found in various areas of the deer's range. Here's a look, north to south, along with insights into hunting techniques in the various habitats.

Kodiak Island, Alaska

This is where the highest Sitka blacktail densities and biggest bucks are found. The terrain varies from a rolling high alpine tundra to steep alder-choked mountainsides to rolling coastline. Until late in the season the bigger bucks are found up high, and you have to climb to get them. When winter approaches and the rut kicks in, they tend to move lower, though they rarely reach the beaches. Generally speaking, spot-and-stalk techniques work best from late October through mid-November; calling and rattling will draw bucks in close.

Southeast Alaska

Dominated by the huge Tongass National Forest, southeast Alaska is a steep, rugged region of old-growth timber laced with small streams, large rivers and lakes of all sizes. There is good deer hunting on the mainland, as well as on many of the area's islands including Prince of Wales and the ABCs—Admiralty, Baranof and Chichagof—where both trophy quality and deer densities are good. Spot-and-stalk techniques apply early, when the deer are in alpine areas above timberline. When the rut kicks in, use doe bleat, fawn distress and grunt calls mixed with judicious rattling inside the thick timber. This is a highly effective technique.

Coastal British Columbia

An extension of southeast Alaska in terms of habitat and hunting style and technique. Good hunting can be found on the mainland, but the best-known and most popular area is Vancouver Island. Deer here are classified as Columbia blacktails, except in the Queen Charlotte Islands, where the deer are classified as Sitka blacktails.

Packing out an Oregon buck. Blacktail country is steep and broken, and you probably won't pull your deer out whole.

Pacific Northwest

The rain forest jungles of coastal Washington and northern Oregon hold good numbers of Columbia blacktails, and some really big bucks. This thick, wet country is often coursed by still-hunters who use logging roads for vehicle access, then poke along on foot. The best jungle hunters approach the game like eastern whitetail hunters, scouting for sign and then setting treestands and ground blinds in the hopes of ambushing a deer.

Calling both vocally and with rattling horns is very effective during the rutting period in November.

Southern Oregon

The steep, timbered mountains of southern Oregon are today's "hot spot" for hunting world-class blacktails. The four-county quadrant of Jackson, Douglas, Coos and Josephine is currently producing the biggest bucks of all, although great bucks are coming from neighboring counties as well. Here a combination of spot-and-stalk and stand-hunting sprinkled with calling and rattling during the rut is the way to go.

Northern California

The giant redwood forests of northern California have produced the most record-book Columbia blacktails. The area is steep, rugged and heavily timbered, with high-country alpine areas and lots of brush thrown in. Backpacking into remote areas is a good way to go, with the Trinity Alps and Marble Mountains Wilderness Area both excellent choices. In both this area and the San Francisco Bay region, many private ranches produce lots of excellent bucks. Bring good optics and be prepared to glass long and hard.

Glassing California blacktail country. California isn't all city—go to where the blacktails are and you'll find big spaces, beautiful country, plenty of deer and good hunting.

Central California Coast

The official southern boundary for the Columbia blacktail runs east/west along the southern borders of Santa Cruz and Santa Clara counties. That said, local deer hunters working San Benito, Monterey and San Luis Obispo counties often erroneously refer to the smallish deer found there as "blacktails," when in truth they are California mule deer. Both these deer and the rugged coastal mountains they inhabit offer a very challenging hunt. With a general rifle season that opens August 10, temperatures can break the century mark. Spot-and-stalk hunting is the way to go here.

SOME FINAL THOUGHTS

There are few big game animals in all of North America more difficult to tie your tag on than a mature Columbia or Sitka blacktail buck. If you think of yourself as a highly skilled hunter, take the blacktail challenge. When you do, you will be humbled like you never thought possible. You'll walk away shaking your head, wondering how in the world such a small package could make such a big fool out of you. And then you'll come back to blacktail country for more, because it, like blacktail hunting, is addictive.

Blacktail Equipment

Shots at blacktails can range from in-your-face close (when hunting thick timber) to way-out-there (when hunting foothills and open hillsides). Classic blacktail rifles are bolt actions chambered for cartridges from the .243 up through the various .300 magnums, the final selection being made with conditions in mind. Quality variable-power scopes make sense even in the thick stuff, with 2-7X, 3-9X, and 2.5-10X all excellent. Stay dialed down to your lowest power setting while hunting, in case you get a quick close-range opportunity.

Standard archery tackle works well for bowhunters, the same gear you'd use on whitetails anywhere. Fiber-optic sight pins are recommended, as shots often occur on the

A bright, fiber-optic sight pin is important in the blacktail woods, which are usually dark, wet and gloomy.

cusp of daylight or under a dark forest canopy. During the late season, rattling and grunt calling can be effective. And these days, more and more savvy Columbia blacktail hunters have found that treestands can be their best friend.

Except for central California, blacktail country is wet. Wearing wool or synthetics like Gore-Tex fleece will keep you warm and quiet, even when wet. I wear a packable Whitewater Outdoors Gore-Tex rain suit when it's raining hard, together with Gore-Tex hunting boots and gloves.

Top quality *fogproof, waterproof* binoculars are critical. Choose 7X to 10X glasses that gather lots of light so you can spot deer at either end of the day, and on those dark, gloomy days that so often characterize blacktail hunting.

Blacktails aren't that different from whitetails—calling and rattling is effective on rutting blacktails too.

Chapter 6

PRONGHORNS: PURE HUNTING FUN

BY TOM CARPENTER

You may work harder for a good whitetail. You'll probably shed more blood and tears pursuing a nice muley. You might dream away a half a lifetime before a truly big elk steps into your sights. But for pure hunting fun, one North American big game animal earns top honors, hands down: our own pronghorn.

What other big game animal lives out where the country is so wide open, offering you the chance to see good numbers of game all day long? What game offers you the chance to get another good shot at a good animal—probably on the same day—if you blow one opportunity? What other hoofed creature (besides a home-grown whitetail) is as affordable to hunt and offers a real chance for a true trophy even to the do-it-yourself hunter? And when you get right down to it, is there any other North American game animal as singularly beautiful and graceful as a pronghorn—all pumpkin-orange and white and black-horned there against the delicate blue-green of the sage?

From the terrain to the animal itself, pursuing pronghorns is an almost magical experience—a low-key, high-enjoyment hunt through the wind and sage, way out there on the prairies and plains and badlands and breaks. And what's wrong with taking the pressure off and just putting some *fun* back into hunting now and again?

Yet just because pronghorn hunting is fun (and success rates high) doesn't mean it's necessarily easy. By its very nature, pronghorn hunting is not as arduous or complicated as packing in to some wilderness area a hundred miles from nowhere.

Just being there, out on the wide-open and lonely prairie, is the essence of pronghorn hunting. Use your own boot leather to get around, and you'll experience a true hunting challenge.

But the challenge comes when you decide to hunt pronghorns fair-and-square—out there in the Wide Open—on foot and on their terms. If you've hunted pronghorns before, you know what I mean. To step out of a truck or off an ATV and pull the trigger is to *shoot* a pronghorn, not *hunt* him.

So here's *how* to hunt him—fairly and efficiently and effectively—with nothing but the sage, hills and wind as your audience … and a true

North American original as your quarry. Pull on a good pair of boots, grab your rifle (or bow, if you so choose), and let's get going.

A CLASSIC RIFLE HUNT

Come on, hop in the truck. We'll eat breakfast on the way, save some time that way. That's a big yawn. Yes I know this is our third day out, and you've heard that pronghorns are civilized and you don't have to be out there at the crack of dawn. But the way we're hunting them, we need to spend every minute we can in the field.

First light—as well as last light—is a perfect time to stalk. Antelope are out feeding, quite visible as they browse along, and their nerves aren't as on-edge as they are when the sun's full-up in the sky. That sun can even offer you some extra cover during a stalk, low in the sky and behind your back and shining into their eyes, if the wind and everything else works out right.

Here. Load your daypack with these sandwiches and some water and juice. I will too. No, we're not cruising around in a truck today either! Your legs are used to it by now. The better bucks aren't anywhere near the two-tracks anyway, and we'll have more fun out there on our own two feet. After each big swing through the prairie, we'll just come back and then drive on to another drainage, get out and work it too. Our first swing, unless we find a good buck, will probably take us a couple hours; it'll be longer if we get on a buck, to get the stalk done right.

Let's get a move on. I'm glad you like those boots, and broke them in back at home … you're out of blister danger! We're going to hike over to that ridge and peek over into that next valley, see what's stirring. It's about a mile over there.

Sneak & Peek

Okay, here we are. Bend your knees and sneak as we creep up to that ridge. We can't just go barging up there and stand out like a sore thumb and glass that valley. Any and every antelope there will be gone. All we'll see are white rumps bouncing over the next ridge.

So let's creep up slowly, peeking over the crest of the ridge bit by bit. You'll see

Only by walking antelope country, sneaking and peeking and never fully exposing yourself to prairie skylines, will you witness the wonder of antelope living their everyday lives. This buck is using his cheek-patch scent glands to mark territory.

new "slivers" of country come into view across the way as we do. Use your binoculars—it's easy to look past an antelope, believe it or not, with your bare eyes.

All right, now we're going to have to get down on our knees and keep going. I don't see any animals yet. They should be here somewhere—they were last night anyway when we sat here at dusk. Antelope usually won't venture far through the night, and you can sometimes come back to the same spot and find them in the morning.

Not here. At least they're not across the way. Oop—stay down. We're not done yet. We haven't seen what's below us yet, on this slope. Let's crawl now, and peek down bit-by-bit. Oh—there they are. They moved this way. They're all does, looks like a smaller band than the group we spotted last night. But I don't see a buck hanging on the fringes.

Planning & Making the Stalk

Here's what we'll do … roll back behind this ridge crest, use it for cover as we sneak down a ways, then creep back up and peek into a new section of the valley. Maybe "our" band moved down toward the waterhole, or maybe we'll find a new bunch.

Here we are. Slow now. Look it all over piece by piece … whoa! There they are, maybe 600 yards out. Here—just poke your head up and take a look. Yes—that's a nice buck, that one on the left. I think he's the only one. Let's take a few minutes and plan a stalk.

How big is he? Well, I'm not that much into inches or scores, but he's a good one. Let me fish my spotting scope out of the pack. Here you go … look how his horns curve beautifully, into a sort of heart shape. That curve will add a lot of length for you. His prong—see how it starts above the ear? That's another good sign. That ear is maybe 6 inches long, he's probably got at least that much horn beyond the prong, and the curve will add 2 or 3 inches more. But most importantly, look how massive those horns are—could you get your thumb and forefinger around the base of one? Maybe. And he's thick all the way up. He's a good buck in anybody's book.

On a good pronghorn stalk, you'll spend a lot of time crawling to take advantage of rises, dips, draws, ditches and other terrain that can cover your approach. Crawling also lets you take advantage of the little bit of vegetation that can help hide you.

What matters most though is that you want him, and I think you do. I thought so. He's a good, mature buck and what more could you ask for?

They're settled in so let's not rush things. A pronghorn group will hang out in a little basin like that all morning. Look at the good feed there—it's a little greener than in the rest of this dry, dusty, sagey country. Must catch some snowmelt as well as summer thundershower drainage. Antelope heaven.

We can't go straight at them—no cover. But if we get around behind them—see that rock outcropping just above a little higher than them but about 150 yards to the east? Yes, that one. That would be a good place to shoot from. We can do it—we're going to have to back off, hike back down the other side of this ridge, then cross over about a mile back where this drainage curves and they can't see us. We'll come down behind the other ridge, drop in that side gully, then creep up to those rocks; mark them good. I'll remember a couple of "checkpoint" landmarks along the way. Here we go.

Closing In, Moments of Truth

Yes, that was a haul. But the wind's right. They're certainly still there. No, I don't want to peek … we're close enough now that they'll bust us if we do. We'll just need to have some faith. Actually, any time you can see an antelope he can see you, only better.

Here, slip on these kneepads, and wear your gloves. We don't want cactus or rocks killing us as we knee-walk, crawl and then slither the last hundred yards. Let's go!

Made it. Let me peek. He's still there. He even fed a little closer, or was chasing a doe and ended up nearer. Let's relax a minute. They don't know we're here, the wind's right, you need to be calm. That was a long, exerting crawl. Let's just watch the sky and clouds for a minute. Here—I'll put this little bleat call in my mouth. If we spook them a little, I'll blat on it and they might hold long enough for you to shoot.

Okay here you go. Just aim for that spot where the back of his front leg meets the line separating the russet orange and white on his chest. You'll

This buck's horns are good in anybody's book: He's got length (look at his horns vs. his ears), good "hooks" at the tips, mass, and deeply forked prongs. Your heart will be pounding big-time as you stalk this fellow.

Edging up over a cutbank and settling in for the shot.

have to use a rest—I have my shooting sticks along but even better will be this rock. I'll put my daypack up there. Our sandwiches might get squashed but they'll make a good cushion! Just joking.

Ease over. Breathe easy. Take your time. Whenever you're ready, just squeeze … good shot! He's hit. Bolt in another shell … oh, he's just teetering around … he's down. Yes, keep your rifle on him. We'll just wait a minute. I know he's done for, but we'll wait to make sure, let things settle down.

Well, let's go see him … oh, my! That's a good buck. Man, look at the thickness of those horns! Here, give 'em a smell—just like sage. Run your hands through that bristly coat. Smells sort of salty, huh? Yes, this is pretty darn fun hunting. And you should be congratulated. We should be. Look. We did it on our own, out here in the middle of all this space. You earned this buck, and should be proud.

Okay, picture time, then let's dress him out. He'll be as fine eating as anything you ever shot—if we take care of him right.

Author Tom Carpenter approaches a nice Montana buck that took more than two hours (including a half-hour belly crawl through a prairie dog town) to stalk.

Hay meadows, alfalfa fields, newly sprouting winter wheat ... agricultural greenery of all types will attract pronghorns. If you have permission and watch out for irrigation and other equipment, these make great places to rifle hunt.

OTHER RIFLE HUNTING METHODS

Sneaking, spotting and stalking is the classic way to rifle-hunt for antelope. But it isn't the only way.

If hunting pressure is fairly heavy and the pronghorns are moving about, wait for a buck to come to you. Choose a place where you can sit comfortably, out of sight—a jumble of rocks or next to a boulder or in a gully cut—and wait. Other good places include passes or saddles between one drainage and another, as well as points of higher land that jut into the flats; as they travel the flats, antelope may skirt these points closely enough for a shot. To locate good stand sites like these, watch a large area from a high vantage point, then move to travel corridors you see antelope using. If you're in ranch country, another good place to sit is at a corner fence; pronghorns will often end up there, herded at one corner of a pasture, when fleeing hunting pressure.

If you're in ranch country and have permission to hunt there, a green meadow or hayfield is a pronghorn magnet. You can wait out first or last light here no matter who you are, and it's a great place to take a younger or older hunter who might not be as mobile out in the sage and rocks.

And don't forget—antelope don't quit drinking during rifle season. You won't have to sit in the close quarters of an archery blind, but you will have to hide out within sure-fire rifle shooting

Binocular Notes

With rifle or bow, you'll spend a lot of hunting time behind a pair of binoculars. The rules are simple. Get good, bright glasses—shop and compare, and go the extra mile to pay for quality. No compacts, period. Get 7 or 8 power (7X35, 8X30 or 8X42 are all good choices). Ten powers will work too if you can hold them steady in the wind. Mark your focus ring so that you can bring the glasses into a standard focus for normal pronghorn-glassing ranges before you bring the binoculars to your eyes; this will greatly reduce eyestrain.

distance (perhaps use a cloth blind, hide in a rock pile or on a gully side again, or even dig a pit if you're real ambitious), or wait on a travel route leading to or from the water.

PRONGHORNS—RIFLE HUNTING WISDOM

No two pronghorn hunts are exactly the same, but the elements are usually very similar. When it comes to spotting and stalking while you're rifle hunting, here are 10 bits of pronghorn-hunting wisdom to keep in mind:

1. Spot the animals before they spot you: Sneak-and-peek around, never exposing yourself fully to any skyline. Keep these words in mind: Bend, creep, sneak, crawl and peek.

Never skyline yourself. Follow terrain that hides you—like the gully in the background here—and creep up to the edge to glass every once in awhile.

2. Once you spot animals, plan your stalk, utilizing "checkpoints" along the way to make sure you're in the right place and on the right track, getting to where you need to be for the shot. Resist the urge to "peek" at the antelope as you close in; they'll spot you.

3. Don't pooh-pooh the wind, or a pronghorn's ears. Pronghorns will smell you and bust you if you're lazy about the wind. Make sure any breeze blows from them to you or, at the least, that your scent isn't drifting toward them. As for their ears—whisper, don't talk; voices carry forever on the prairie. And wear quiet clothing such as wool or fleece or some newfangled miracle fabric that is cushy and quiet … whatever will make little to no noise scraping over rocks and against sage, bitterbrush, rabbitbrush, grass and other vegetation as you stalk.

4. Remember that exposing yourself to the pronghorn's unbelievably sharp eyes will blow your cover every time. Take the time to stalk carefully, and use the terrain to stay out of sight.

This buck is curious, has you spotted and is ready to explode. Don't move one iota! He just might go about his business, or even get curious and approach a little closer.

5. Don't rush your shot. If you've stalked well, the animals should be calm and still.

6. Wait for the right shot. The hardest thing you might have to do now is wait for other animals to clear from in front of and behind the antelope you want to shoot.

7. Don't shoot at a running pronghorn. You'll hit one you don't want, or worse yet, make a bad hit. You definitely don't want that—not in this country, not on a tenacious pronghorn.

8. Use a rest for your shot (see page 103).

9. Don't despair if you spook a band or miss a shot and send them running. You could get another shot that same day, if you don't push them too hard. At the very least, there will be some other animals around to hunt, dispersed about the prairie habitat.

10. Believe it or not, pronghorns are homebodies and will frequently come back to a piece of habitat they like. Wait right there all day if you have to. If you miss one, they'll loop back—often in a fairly short while.

BOWHUNTING PRONGHORNS

I love hunting pronghorns with a rifle. And, doing it fair-and-square, the hunt is full of challenge. Once you try to stalk within rifle range of a wary band of pronghorns though, you might wonder how someone would ever get close enough to shoot one with a bow and arrow. It's not impossible! In fact, bowhunters do it every year in antelope country.

Most archery pronghorns are taken from blinds set at waterholes. But another super-exciting and effective technique, one that gets archers out on the prairie and not waiting behind burlap or in a plywood-covered pit, is decoy hunting

Antelope often travel in groups, so you may face the challenge of waiting for other animals to clear away from the one you want to shoot. Pull the trigger on this buck now and you'll likely have a dead doe on your hands too—not good if you only have one tag. Have patience!

Pronghorn Field Care

Good field care is important for any big game animal you shoot, but prompt and proper attention is especially crucial when it comes to pronghorns. Why? Because both bow and rifle antelope hunts are often held when the weather is warm, and because antelope are thick-bodied, heavily muscled animals for their size; couple all that with their insulating hair, and you have a cooling challenge on your hands.

Field dress the animal as soon as possible, after a quick picture session. Drain all blood. Try to get the carcass into some shade to start it cooling. Wash the cavity with water if you can, to remove blood and other juices from the meat. Skin the animal in the field if possible (use a tarp or the pronghorn's skin to keep things clean as you work), and put the carcass in a cheesecloth-type game bag to keep flies off the meat. Short of skinning, if the temperatures are much above 50°F or so, get the animal to a locker plant for skinning and cooling as quickly as possible.

Properly attended to, a pronghorn furnishes meat as sweet and delightful as any game, anywhere. It's not deer, it's not elk. Like the animal that produced it, pronghorn meat is its own thing. Someone who tells you they choked down bad pronghorn meat was eating one that wasn't taken care of properly. Even a rutting buck is good if you treat it right.

Admire him a minute, take your pictures, and then start the field-dressing process promptly.

When hunting a waterhole blind with archery gear, draw your bow only when his head is down and the slurping and gulping has begun.

during the rut. Finally, a few hard-core technique traditionalists go after pronghorns by spotting and stalking.

Waterhole Hunting

My first archery pronghorn came at a waterhole, and the setup was pretty typical. My good friend's huge, central Wyoming pasture was home to several pronghorn groups, and they regularly used a watering hole (fed by a well and made for cattle) up on a hilltop. The blind was actually a triangular-shaped pit enclosed by plywood painted the tan color of the prairie. One side, with a shooting porthole, faced the water; peep-

holes looked out the blind's other two sides, so I could peek out and see what was coming from other directions.

On my second day of waiting, two bucks came in mid-morning and drank at the tiny pond's far end. I couldn't angle a shot out the porthole. When they left, I happened to look out one of the blind's peepholes, and another buck was walking in from behind within spitting distance! I grabbed my bow, prepared to shoot, looked out the porthole, and there he was.

The first arrow whizzed over his back but both he and I were undaunted. He came back for his drink, I nocked another arrow and … missed again! Hands shaking, I thought maybe the third time's a charm, and it was—except on a different buck. This one strolled in front of the shooting window so I just pulled back and let go. All I could see was antelope chest so I couldn't miss that shot, and didn't. I scrambled up and out of the blind's door to see a buck and does trotting over the hill, but then I looked the other direction, across the tiny pond, to see my buck staggering and then fall for good, a mere 30 yards away.

Waterhole hunting is simple but fun. You'll probably have to hire an outfitter to coordinate your hunt. Once you're in the blind, prepare for an all-day wait. Be patient. Take in plenty of food and drink, and a book or magazines to read. You'll also see a lot of wildlife; I've had mule deer, coyotes, a badger, porcupines, skunks, sage hens and innumerable songbirds, including electric-blue mountain bluebirds, entertain me during waterhole waits.

And sooner or later, a band of antelope will top a rise way over yonder and start drifting your way. You'll grab your bow and feel your heart race and the blood pound through your head as the antelope wander in your general direction. Then they might even come full-speed ahead, thinking the coast is clear, and you'll wonder how they can't hear the throbbing of your heart as you pick out the animal you want, wait for the others to clear, and draw your bow. Then it's up to you to make the shot.

The author with a good buck pronghorn taken at a Wyoming waterhole. Note the pond and hunting blind in the background.

Understanding Pronghorns

Pronghorns are fast—faster, for any distance longer than the hundred-yard dash, than any other animal on earth.

Our pronghorn, *Antilocapra americana*, is not related to any other game animal on our continent, or the globe, for that matter. He evolved right here, on our North American Plains, and roamed here when the last dinosaurs did, as well as giant cheetahs and huge sabre-toothed cats.

We also call him antelope, and that's okay too. The first explorers dubbed him that, because they thought he resembled the Old World antelopes. But he's better—faster to be sure, the fastest animal on earth for any distance. Top pronghorn speeds range from estimates of 45 to 65 miles per hour. I believe in the upper end of that range, for short bursts, and know that a pronghorn can run at a 35 to 45 mph clip almost forever. (For comparison, 30 mph is top whitetail speed.) The only things that limit the distance pronghorns can run are the fences we have added to the West.

Why are pronghorns so fast, faster by far than any of today's predators? Because pronghorns evolved out there with those huge and speedy but now-extinct cats. Pronghorns persisted and have lost at most only a notch or two of speed in the evolutionary blink of time since.

A mature buck weighs anywhere from 100 to 140 pounds on the hoof. A good buck in a good area will probably be 110 to 130 pounds. Does average a bit smaller—maybe 100 pounds or a little less.

Pronghorns browse for their forage—like deer—and are not grazers (grass eaters). Feeding studies show that little grass is consumed except early in spring, at first green-up. This explains why pronghorns are most numerous in sage country (where

Antelope are grazers, eating browse such as sage and rabbitbrush, along with succulent forbs and weeds they can find. Grasses are low on the food priority scale.

shrubs and forbs dominate the diet), and less common in pure grassland or cropland habitat. But antelope love a good green field of alfalfa, winter wheat or other agricultural crops when available; any green, succulent food is relished. Pronghorn habitat is relatively high altitude (4,000 to 6,000 feet or even a little more) and usually considered a desert, with only 8 to 15 inches of precipitation a year.

Pronghorn hair is hollow—a perfect insulator against the winter cold, wind and snow. To cool him on a hot summer day, a special set of muscles just below the skin allow an antelope to ruffle this hair so the summer breezes can blow through and cool his skin.

The rump hair is long—3 to 5 inches—and bright white. An alarmed pronghorn will flair this beacon, and it is visible for miles as a warning to other pronghorns ... and yes, to you, as if to say, "give it up!"

The objects of hunters' affections—those handsome horns—actually shed every year. A buck's black horn sheath comes off every November, and the new horn grows over the next winter and early summer. The horns are not hair, but a keratin-like substance, much like your fingernails. In a late season you might shoot a pronghorn buck and one or both horns will pop off when he falls!

The horns are ready for use by September, when bucks battle during the rut. Bucks prefer to defend a territory and breed the does within it. But where human activity, hunting pressure or fragmented habitat keeps herds on the move, a buck will gather a harem and stay on the move with it, defending against

all comers his right to breed does. This is a lot more work than patrolling and defending a territory.

Antelope fawns (often twins, on good range) are born in early June, and can run fast enough to escape predators only a couple days later. But coyotes can devastate young fawn populations—efficiently ferreting out the youngest hiders as a doe tries to feign an injury to lure the predator away.

Pronghorn vision is extraordinary and has been likened to 8X binoculars. Plus, bulging eyes let an antelope see literally behind himself except for a very narrow cone right behind the head. Those eyes catch every bit of movement out there on the prairie—everything. Pronghorn hearing is wonderful too, and so is their sense of smell. Although you might not need to wear a scent-lock suit while pronghorn hunting, you're foolish to hunt or stalk with the wind, or ignore it in any other hunting situation.

Pronghorns are curious animals. Sometimes you can get by with a mistake or two while hunting, because they'll wonder what's up and hang around or even come closer to you to see what's going on. But more often they're just spooky and nervous, not likely to wait around if you let them see, smell or hear you. All you'll see are those big white rumps bouncing a big, bright good-bye.

The horns of a mature buck antelope fork midway or so up the beam, forming the prong, and curve gracefully inward or backward at the tips (right). This is the only horned mammal that sheds its horns—actually sheaths (above)—every year. A bony core protrudes from the skull, and that's what the horns grow on.

Sneak within a hundred yards or so, raise up your decoy, squat behind it and blow a snort-wheeze challenge call (above). If a buck's in the right mood, he will come in very quickly and aggressively (right).

Bowhunting with Decoys

If you want to shoot an antelope with your bow, then waterhole hunting is your best bet. But if you've done that before, you're not very patient, you're after some extra excitement or some combination thereof, then try hunting rutting bucks with a decoy. This is an archery-only proposition, since you don't want to be around a lifelike antelope replica of any kind, anywhere (public or private land) when rifle season is open.

Like other antelope pursuit, decoy hunting is a relatively simple proposition. Other than good camouflage for the prairie (usually lighter-brown and tan garb, and don't forget facepaint or a head-

net) and your bow and arrow, you'll need a decoy and a snort-wheeze call (see sidebar below).

The idea is this. A rutting buck, whether he is defending a breeding territory or a harem, wants to run off a potential competing buck (your decoy). So search the prairie as you would when rifle hunting (see first section of this story) to find

a band of does and their attending buck. Put on a stalk or try to intercept them, with the goal of getting within say 100 yards, while staying out of sight and keeping the wind in your favor.

Creep up to a rise, raise the decoy so the buck sees it, and blow a challenge call. If everything is working just so and his mood is right, the buck will charge in to kick the challenger's behind and

Antelope Decoys & Calls

One of the best decoys for spot-and-stalk hunting is the Dutton (Box 113, Faith, SD 57626, 605-967-2031). It's lifelike, lightweight, and folds up into an easy-carry package. As for calls, my best luck has always been with the Lohman "Antelope Challenge" Call (Box 220, Neosho, MO 64850, 417-451-4438 or 800-922-9034). If you haven't heard pronghorn bucks snorting and wheezing and "chuckling" and challenging one another—they're really quite vocal creatures—get a cassette tape too. This is the easiest call in the world to blow. I also like to carry an E.L.K. Inc. "Antelope Talk" Call (Box 85, Gardiner, MT 59030, 406-848-7655 or 800-272-4355) in my mouth while stalking.

chase him off. You need to be hiding just far enough behind your decoy that you can draw your bow back there as the buck comes in. Then rise up, with bow at full draw, to shoot. A buck will give you a couple split seconds to aim and release before he figures out something is wrong.

Putting up a decoy doesn't work every time. Some bucks will just herd their harem over a different hill when the decoy pops up. Other bucks will watch it closely, maybe circle it stiff-legged from far away, but never come near. Others won't pay it any attention at all. But sooner or later, if you keep trying, you'll get a snorting, stomping buck antelope coming straight in and, once again, you'll wonder if your heart can take all the pounding and racing you're subjecting it to.

Spot & Stalk (or Ambush) Archery Hunting

A very small but very dedicated group of pronghorn bowhunters lives and dies by traditional spot-and-stalk methods: sneaking around the prairie, creeping up to peek over hills and rises, looking for a group of antelope that can be circled and approached from behind the cover of topography. More effective, though, might be this variation: the spot-and-ambush. The reason it works better is that a moving pronghorn has more to worry about than just spotting your camouflaged body wallow-

Stalking into bow range of an antelope is about as tough a hunting challenge as you will find anywhere.

ing through the sage. Find a group, wait until they get up to move, guess their direction of travel, then play the wind right and get ahead to an ambush spot. My friend Dave Tieszen, a South Dakotan, is one of the few people I know who have ever taken an antelope this way, and he's done it several times. The fact that he's a very good bow shot helps.

As soon as he steps behind the rise, this buck is in perfect position for the final approach. Skedaddle over there quickly and quietly, and have your bow drawn when you peek over.

A buck antelope surveying his prairie territory. This isn't a huge buck, but like any antelope, he would be a true trophy for any hunter who chooses to hunt fair-and-square.

Bows for Pronghorns

Pronghorns aren't huge, and their skin is relatively thin, so you don't need to over-bow yourself, especially if you'll be waterhole hunting. That first waterhole buck of mine? I shot him with a 20-year-old Bear Whitetail compound that had its wheels on brackets. Did the job fine. So really, any good compound will work. Set your peak draw weight at 50 pounds or above, but you could get by with 45 or so. Remember—you can't over-kill them, so use a higher draw weight if that's what you're comfortable with and used to. Use a fixed-blade broadhead—every Satellite I have sent through a pronghorn has come out the other side perfectly intact. Sight in according to your outfitter's instructions for a waterhole hunt; chances are your shot will be 15 to 20 yards. If you're decoy or spot-and-stalk hunting, be prepared for 10-, 20- and 30-yard shots … 40 if you can swing it consistently. Most importantly, know your range, limit yourself to it, and practice judging distances in open spaces.

Antelope country is big, open, lonely ... as lovely a place as you could ask for.

THE REWARDS

It just feels good to hunt antelope—with rifle or bow in hand, or even a muzzleloader for that matter. With all the gadgetry and gizmos and complications we have added to our various styles of hunting these days—even to our lives—it's nice to know something simple and fun and rewarding still exists.

With just a few good strategies, something to shoot with, good binoculars and a willing pair of legs, you really can feel good about your hunting skills—finding, getting close to and then shooting an antelope out there in the immensity of the prairie, with nothing but an ocean of blue sky above and a rolling sea of sage and grass all around you. Buck or doe, big or small, I ceased to care long ago which particular animal I shot. It's the being there and doing it, out there on the prairie in the middle of nothing and of everything, that matters. 🦌

Rifles for Pronghorns

The perfect pronghorn rifle? Bolt action. Scoped—I prefer a variable power in a medium power range, let's say 2X to 7X. Caliber? .30-06 is what I use, for versatility on other game. If I could afford a pronghorn-only rifle, it would be a .270: fast and flat-shooting. Cartridges? Use a good, fast boat-tail bullet; I like a 165-grainer because it seems to buck the ever-present prairie wind better, but a 150-grain or even a 130-grain bullet (in the .270) would do the job. On that .30-06 or .270, sight in about 2.5 inches (no more) high at 100 yards, and you'll be able to hold right on a buck's chest on out to about 250 to 275 yards. I don't want or need to shoot farther than that anyway. A sling is a necessary accessory for carrying your rifle long distances and snuggling in tight for the shot.

Always use a rest of some type in pronghorn country. Four variations are shown below—a bipod right on your rifle, shooting sticks, a pack laid on either the ground or a rock, or use a fencepost or anything else available. Just don't shoot offhand. Shooting prone is tough; in good pronghorn country, sage and shrubs will get in the way.

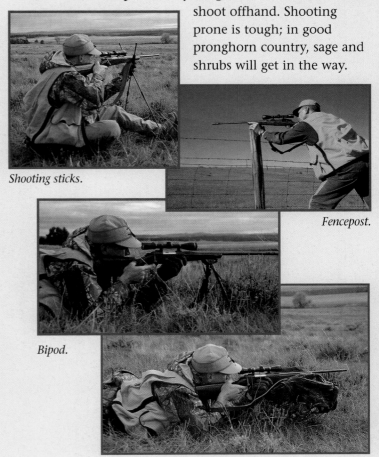

Shooting sticks.

Fencepost.

Bipod.

Pack over the sage.

Chapter 7

BEARS: GAME THAT CAN HUNT BACK

BY JIM SHOCKEY

Dawn at the best of times rises gently out of the night, unfurling like a morning flower to bring light to a dark world. The deer hunter will have seen this dawn and know it for a time of quietude, a time of respectful silence, a time just before first light when no animal moves, out of reverence for the beginning of the new day. Dawn at the best of times is as beautiful and serene as a whispered promise.

But there is another dawn, not gentle, not at all like an unfurling flower. This dawn crawls out of the night like an evil thing. It slides slowly across the land, sinister and bloated with a fog that turns black to gray and promises nothing but ill. This dawn the hunter will know well too, for this is the dawn of dampness and cold and of shivering apprehension.

This is the dawn of the bear hunter.

I hunched my shoulders against the mist, trying to block the damp from seeping farther down inside the back of my shirt. The fog bumped and swirled around me, set to motion by the tiny movement I'd made. A salmon flopped on the surface frightening another which rocketed up the river unseen but for the watery swell over its humped back. I was hidden and leaning against a cutbank, standing in a pool of water to my knees. At my feet a dozen salmon prepared nests by lying on their sides and digging down into the gravel with their tails.

At the bottom of the pool a dozen more salmon finned quietly, awaiting the slow malignant death of the leper. They were done breeding, done with their lives. Their fins were white and rotting and their once sleek and silver sides were now mottled with horrible white sores. Every quarter hour, one of these grotesque creatures would turn sideways to the current and then, without so much as a passing regret, give up and die, letting the current deliver the rotting flesh where it would.

Though I couldn't see far enough upstream through the fog to confirm it, the lifeless carcasses floating past in front of me told of a

Black bears eat salmon too, just like the grizzlies and browns you usually hear about. And when the hunting quarters are this close, your adrenaline will be pumping.

thousand salmon breeding and dying in the pools upstream from where I stood. Probably it was the morbidity of that knowledge, life begetting death, begetting life, begetting death, that made the fog seem like it was hanging heavy around me like a sinister foreshadowing pall.

Something bumped my hip-wader and I startled. My heart pounded uncontrollably, disregarding the message my wide eyes relayed. It was just a dead salmon.

Black bears (which I was hunting) are just as dangerous as grizzlies and brown bears, because the blacks are dangerously underestimated by most hunters. It isn't until you hunt them on the ground and on their terms that you start to take them seriously and that you truly learn what they are capable of. Two years before, one of my guides had been mauled by a black bear that a client had wounded. And every year my guides and I find ourselves face to face with a problem bruin.

A salmon splashed several yards away in a deep pool and a raven croaked somewhere out of sight down the stream. A smaller bird of some descrip-

tion started singing in a soft song in contrast to the raven. No doubt the smaller bird was on its way south. Another salmon jumped close by.

My heart rate was only just beginning to return to normal when it happened. One second the stream ahead was just a stream and the next second it was a stream with a huge black leg stepping into it. A bear! And a big one by the looks of the leg. The leg had appeared from out of the thick underbrush choking the side of the stream. I couldn't see anything above the bear's elbow because my vision was obscured by dead snag angling out from the side of the stream fifty yards away. The bear might have been another ten yards past the tree but I couldn't be sure.

Another second passed and then two more before the first leg was joined by another. Once again my heart started pounding wildly and my breathing became ragged. The morning to that point had been hard enough on the nerves but now I was faced with controlling those frazzled nerves for a further and indeterminate length of time.

The bear couldn't have seen me any better than I could see him but I had the advantage. He was moving. I was still. He stepped from the bank and waded to an exposed gravel bar midstream. The ocean tide had been receding all morning, dropping the depth of water in the stream even as far from the ocean as we were. The bear knew this and was coming down to the stream to feed on the corpses of any salmon caught in the riffles along the gravel bar. He'd probably been feeding that way undisturbed for most of his 15 years. He had no reason to expect a hunter to be there.

But I was there.

They say a bear's sight is poor and in some respects that is right but when that old boar stepped into the open around the broken trunk of that overhanging snag, he picked me up instantaneously.

He didn't run and I didn't rush my shot.

We both knew the score.

So does the dawn rise for the bear hunter?

General Judging Tips for "Big" Bears

In all the many years I've outfitted for bears, not one of my client hunters has told me that his dream was to shoot a small bear. It hasn't happened and it never will. The fascination we hunters have with big bears is ancient and primal, a combination of fear and facing that fear. It's akin to climbing up onto the roof of a building and looking down over the edge. The higher the building (the bigger the bear), the deeper the fascination.

So why is it that most hunters have small or medium-sized black bearskin rugs on their wall? Why indeed. Most will say something to the effect of: "He (or she) looked huge to me."

The toughest part of taking a big black bear is knowing what "big" looks like. Here are some general tips to help in judging bears:

Location

Big bears live, eat and hang out in the best living, eating and hanging-out areas. Find the best-looking bear habitat in the hunting area and odds are the bear you see there will be big—especially during prime evening hours. Small bears usually live in marginal habitat for their own safety: Big bears eat small bears.

Attitude

Big bears are the toughest, meanest sons-of-guns in the valley and they act it. Watch a human bully walk down the street. He walks with a swagger and an attitude. A big bear walks the same way. He doesn't fit and start at every sound like a small bear will. A big bear doesn't have to; he believes he's got nothing to fear.

Scale

A big bear looks big ... but so does a closer, smaller bear. Here's a quantitative example of this. If the bear is 200 yards away but the hunter thinks the bear is 250 yards away, the hunter will overestimate the bear's relative size by 25 percent. In other words, the hunter is in for a serious case of ground shrink when he walks up to his bear. Get as close to the bear as you can. The closer the bear, the less chance there is of misjudging the distance to the bear and thereby misjudging the bear's relative size.

Is he a big one or isn't he? Get close to take a good look.

Bears with Personality

Fuzzy Teddy Bear or Ferocious Menace? Man eating or good eating? Endangered animal or common backyard pest? Big game trophy, bumbling clown or wilderness icon? Rug or cure for arthritis? Provider of claws for ceremony or provider of wildlife viewing opportunity?

Which is it? The fact is, the four species of bear in North America—the black bear, the grizzly, the brown bear and the polar bears of the Far North—are all of the above. They have multiple personalities. They are the "Sybils" of the animal kingdom. Take the black bear for example. Even calling one black is a contradiction in terms; they can be black, blue, brown, red, cinnamon, blond and even, in the case of the much-vaunted Kermode bear, white.

Personality disorders aside, all bears of late have found themselves thrust into the hunting limelight. Not only because several times a year they find themselves gracing the front pages for mutilating and/or eating some unfortunate human being, but because bear hunting is becoming more popular.

So what's the fatal attraction? Why are more hunters looking for these potentially dangerous animals than ever before? The short answer is, because bears bite. It's a kind of fatal attraction that lures hunters away from the safety of their deer stands and into the high adventure of the typical bear hunt. No matter which way a hunter chooses to hunt, either over bait, following hound dogs or spotting and stalking, no matter which way a bear hunt is cut, it's exciting. Better still, in many places, it is a hunt that takes place in the spring, and therefore does not interfere with most "traditional" big game hunts that occur in autumn.

Black bears can get ornery too, just like their big brown and grizzly cousins.

Big Game Wisdom

SPECIFIC TIPS FOR JUDGING "BIG" BEARS

If the bear fails any one of the listed general judgments, then it would be wise to let him walk. Chances are it's not a big bear. On the other hand, if it passes all the initial criteria, then it's time to get serious about judging the bear's size. Keep reading to find out how.

Body Shape

Do you wear the same size pants as you did when you were in high school? Be honest; does your spouse poke you in the belly once in a while and tell you to cut back on the Twinkies? Bigger bears are older bears, and like most of us, they don't have the svelte bodies they once did. They

This guy has all the characteristics of a big bear: massive legs, hump over the shoulder, broad head, ears pointing to the side.

tend to look "heavy" and out of shape. Remember, they monopolize the best feed and habitat and, therefore, expend less energy to live.

Head Shape

A big boar bear will have a deeper, wider and longer snout than a smaller bear or a female bear. His ears will seem to be wide apart and small. If he is aware of you and looking your way, his ears won't stand up on top of his head like a dog's ears, they'll seem to be aimed out to the side of his head. A big bear will have well-developed, even bulging, biting muscles behind his forehead.

Legs

A big bear will have massively developed front shoulders. His shoulders will look big like a wrestler's. A sow's wrist will pinch in directly above the foot. Not so with a boar: The lower forearm, wrist and the foot on a big boar are all the same width. A big bear often appears to have shorter legs because the body is so much thicker. But keep in mind that the best-scoring bears for the record book are often the lankier looking, longer bodied bears.

MISTAKES BEAR HUNTERS MAKE

Bear hunting, like any type of hunting, has its own set of myths and misconceptions that go with it. Here are some common mistakes inexperienced bear hunters make, and some ideas for doing things right instead.

Point of Aim

Many hunters read the articles that tell them to bust the bear down and shoot at the shoulder. That's writer advice. My advice and the advice of every single bear outfitter I've ever talked to, or at least the ones who outfit for more than 40 bears per year, is to aim for the lungs. Every bear shot through the lungs dies quickly and humanely and is always recovered. Not so for bears with broken shoulders.

Control any fear and make your first shot count.

Controlling Fear

Black bears and the vast majority of "big bears" do not generally charge at the shot or before the shot. Yet the stories told most often around the campfire are the bear attack stories. It does happen, but not nearly so often as it happens around the campfire. If there is going to be a problem, it'll be after a bad shot. Stories are just that: stories. Forget the "getting charged" hype and concentrate on making a good shot.

Use Enough Gun

I can't count how many times I've heard hunters telling me that their .30-30 Winchester is all the black bear medicine a guy needs. These hunters are right—for small bears. But for big bears, they're wrong. I know, I'm the guy who gets

gray hair crawling around in the "thick stuff" looking for their wounded bears.

On a big bear, of the 400-pound-plus variety, and in spite of what the late Jack O'Conner would have you believe, a .270 Winchester is the barest minimum caliber the average hunter should consider. And such a small rifle or muzzleloader should only be fired if the bear presents a perfect shot. Sorry all you Jack fans, but you won't bust through the thick part of a bear to its vitals with a .270 Winchester. Do yourself and that "biggest bear of your life" a favor. Pick up a bolt-action .300 Winchester or .338 Winchester, or be prepared to pass up marginal shots.

Give Them Credit

Many bears are alive today because the hunters pursuing them didn't give enough credit to the bears for their senses. Yes, they have incredible noses, better by a measure than a white-tailed deer, but they also have excellent hearing and, though most won't believe it, eyesight too. They don't see motionless hunters well, but they pick up movement easily and at great distances. Depending on how actively the bear has been hunted, they'll disappear like ghosts at the barest hint of danger.

Bears are smart. Very smart. This one knows you are there and will be gone in the time it takes you to blink.

BEAR HUNTING STRATEGIES

Different bears and different habitats require different hunting strategies. Here's a rundown.

Hunting Using Bait (Black Bears Only)

By far and away, where it's legal, the method of choice for most black bear hunting is baiting. This strategy is most popular because it is the only way to hunt black bears in most areas. Typically, the bait is set out early in the spring when the bears are first coming out of hibernation. As they search the countryside for the first bits of food, bears happen upon the baits and hopefully into the waiting hunter's crosshairs. This spring hunting is common in Canada. In the U.S. bear states, bait hunting usually occurs in autumn while the bears are stoking up for winter.

Bear hunter climbing up into his stand to begin his vigil.

This hunt, despite its passive qualities, is a good hunt in the sense that it allows the hunter to determine the size of the bear accurately and also to pick and choose the shot. Generally, you're situated in a treestand of some description and have ample time to judge the bear.

The actual bait used varies. Apples, old bread and pastries, beaver carcasses, oats, wheat, corn, molasses, icing sugar, restaurant food scraps and waste … the more odoriferous the better! Bear hunters all have their own secret recipes for bear bait.

Hunting Using Hounds (Black Bears Only)

Although the practice is not as popular as it once was, chasing bears with hounds is still a viable way to hunt bears. (Be sure to check your area's regulations first.) Usually the dogs are used to "strike" a track before being released on the trail. The hunt is a wild chase on foot through some of the most "human-resistant" cover available to the bear. In the end, the bear is either treed or it bays up long enough for the hunter to catch up to the action and decide if the bear is large enough to shoot.

Black bear coming in to a bait station.

A treed black bear. The adventure is in the chase, and this is a type of hunting that truly can be catch-and-release!

Of all the hunting techniques, hunting with hounds is the closest hunters will ever come to "catch-and-release" hunting: All you have to do is decide not to pull the trigger and *voilá*—both the bear and you live to run the chase again.

Hunting Tidal Flats (Black, Grizzly and Brown Bears)

Along the Northwest coast (Canada and Alaska), the bear hunting begins on or around April 1st. The south-facing slopes are just greening up by then and the fresh growth is a magnet for the bruins. They require the greenery to kick start their digestive system into gear after several months of inactivity. Likewise, the tidal flats found at the mouth of every river and creek act as bear magnets.

You'll need a small boat to get into the shallow tidal flats where early-spring bears congregate.

Tidal flat hunting is as exciting as anything you'll ever do. You'll need to be stealthy enough to wade quietly (left) and prepared to come upon a huge, feeding bruin (below) in a fraction of a moment as you round a bend or creep up to a run-off channel at low tide.

Hunting bears anywhere is exciting, but hunting the tidal flats can be especially so. The tidal flats look like pancakes but in fact they are criss-crossed by deep run-off channels. And it is in these deep ditches that the bears prefer to feed. As the ocean waters recede to the low tide mark, fresh greens down in the muddy channels are left exposed, like so many nutrient-filled asparagus tips.

Generally, access to these grassy flats is by boat only and the ride is a treat in and of itself. It isn't unusual to see sea otters, elephant seals, sea lions and the occasional killer whale.

bears are huntable in the thickest of forests. But where baiting is not allowed, the only way the big bears living in the thick forest can be hunted is by waiting for the rut. For it is during this time that they come out on to old overgrown logging roads and mark their territory.

Bears "bust branches" when they rut. For all intents and purposes, it is the male black bear's equivalent of a whitetail buck's rubs and scrapes. The big bears will work their way down a trail or old road, stopping every few feet to destroy saplings. The boar will stand up on his hind legs and reach over its shoulder and grab the stem of the 10- or 12-foot sapling. Then the bear will pull the sapling over his shoulder and bite the stem, breaking it. The bear will then trash the broken tree's branches and leaves before walking on to the next tree.

It's spring and he's out looking for some action: This is the time to hunt rutting bruins.

Hunting the Rut (Black, Grizzly and Brown Bears)

In the last two weeks in May and the first week of June, the bear rut kicks into high gear. Big boars begin wandering all over the countryside looking for female bears. And when you have animals moving of their own accord, you have excellent hunting opportunities. Whether the hunter is on stand in the northern forest or glassing logged-off areas, the bears are just plain easier to find.

In places where baiting is allowed, the biggest

Bruins leave calling cards in the form of busted branches and saplings. Scout for this sign.

Where to Go: Best Bets for Big Bear

Bear country is invariably big, wild and beautiful—a place you'll love to be. This is Kodiak Island, Alaska.

Without a doubt, the best place to hunt big black bears is off the west coast of British Columbia on Vancouver Island. The bears there are huge and abundant, albeit only in the black phase. The best bet for colored black bears is the interior of British Columbia, Alberta or Saskatchewan. All these provinces produce the odd giant black bear. In British Columbia, baiting is illegal and all hunts are spot-and-stalk or hound hunts. The other provinces allow baiting. Alaska offers some excellent black bear hunting but the costs to get to the best areas can be prohibitive. The cheapest hunts take place in Quebec and the Eastern Canadian provinces, but success is low.

In general, bear hunting below the 49th parallel isn't quite as easy as it is in Canada and Alaska, except in a few of the Rocky Mountain States. The northern reaches of Minnesota, Wisconsin and Michigan have fairly good bear populations. Some big ones are taken, but it's nothing like in Canada.

There is the odd large boar killed in the East or Upper Midwest, but tags are often difficult to obtain.

The best places to hunt grizzlies are British Columbia, Alaska, Yukon and the Northwest Territories. All these hunts are spot-and-stalk and can take place from the coastal salmon streams to the tundra of the central Arctic.

Genetically identical to the brown bears of coastal Alaska, the largest grizzlies are taken along the coast of British Columbia. That said, anywhere along the "political" boundary between where brown bears become grizzlies is a good place to hunt for big silvertips.

Traditionally, the largest brown bears are found on Kodiak Island but of late, several monster bears have been taken from the tip of the Alaska Peninsula. These huge mammals are hunted in the spring and fall along salmon streams, berry patches or green slides. The weather is often a factor on a brown bear hunt: Hunters can expect rain, rain and more rain interspersed with gale-force winds. Nice.

Polar bears are still hunted in the Northwest Territories by the Inuit trappers and by lucky sport hunters. These bears must be hunted from a dogsled pulled by a dog team. This hunt is a true adventure that shouldn't be considered by the faint of heart. Temperatures range to a low of minus 50°F with wind-chill factors falling to minus 100! Only polar bears taken from certain areas are allowed to be imported into the United States.

It's a different feeling, hunting the big bears, because they can hunt you back.

THE "BIG" BEARS

The big grizzly appeared to be a black, silver-tipped speck in the spotting scope. It seemed easy and sure; just watch him until dark, sleep, and then pick him up in the morning again. The bear wouldn't go far: He was ankle-deep in a heavenly moss berry patch. The big boar might as well have been standing in jam.

Nor did he go far. At first light the bear was right back in the thick of the berry patch, chowing down on the calorie-laden sweets. Elvis at his hungriest would have been humbled by the big bear's intake. As he gobbled, I made a plan. Ha! What work? All I had to do was cross the river here, climb through that drainage there, pick my way through a thousand vertical feet of dog-hair alders, then poke my head up by that lichened yellow boulder and there he should stand!

I'd tell you about wading the icy water, my gun tied to my backpack, my hands free to double grip the stiff walking stick and about climbing the slick mountainside, but I won't. And I won't tell you about poking my schnauze over the edge of the hanging basin and discovering the grizzly was gone. I will, however, tell you the only thing worse than a found grizzly is a missing grizzly. Truly, human significance ebbs lowest in that moment when a grizzly bear hunter realizes that perhaps his and his quarry's roles have been reversed. Where the heck was the grizzly?

The green and yellow alder-clad mountains sloped away on three sides, dangling over the edge of the hidden basin where I fretted. As is usual when hunting in the mountains, what I thought I'd seen from the bottom through my spotting scope, wasn't. Instead of the small fold I expected to find beyond the ridge where the bear had been, there was a large basin; a basin choked with alder patches. The bear could be anywhere, close by or far. The wind swirled, I shivered, then started. Bear! Not 200 yards away, a blond grizzly appeared from behind a clump of alders.

Blond grizzly? I frowned. The bear I'd seen was a much larger, black-colored silvertip! But before I had time to mouth "uh oh" a second bear appeared, and then a third! Nearly as large as the blond one, the two new bears were obviously adolescents. That said, at 300 or so pounds each, either would be a handful in a scuffle. If the sow

Grizzly hunting is done in some magnificent settings.

Here's the author, Jim Shockey, with a very large British Columbia silvertip grizzly bear.

came wading into the fray, I'd be little more than a mouthful.

Go figure, but all of a sudden I began questioning the logic of hanging out in the middle of the largest berry patch on the mountain by myself. Probably at that point, I would have slipped out the back door, the same way I let myself in, but when I turned to look, a fourth grizzly lumbered into sight! This one came from behind and below me and although it was certainly a boar, again it wasn't the bear I was hunting! Visions of a search party retrieving my spit-covered body—if there was anything left to retrieve—filled my mind's eye.

Suddenly grizzly bear hunting was exactly the hard work I knew it would be. Let me see, 45 seconds to reload my Knight muzzleloader and, assuming I managed to kill the first bear, I figured it would take the other three bears about five seconds flat to get to me. That would leave about 40 seconds for the three of them to enjoy their meal before I could get off a second shot. In other words, I'd be a bear burp before I could reload.

That's about the instant I saw "my" bear, the fifth of the sloth, ambling through the alders. By some quirk of mountain updrafts, downdrafts,

crossdrafts and currents, none of the beasts had smelled me yet. The sow however, instantly lifted her nose to the wind when the big bear appeared. "Woof!" The sow bolted, cubs in tow. My odds were improving.

A few minutes later they improved again when the big silvertip did his dominant thing and aggressively displayed the remaining bear into the next mountain range.

Good move for the smaller bear, bad for the bigger. Now the odds were more even. I waited until the boar fed his way to within 60 yards, close enough for a humane killing shot but far enough away to be safe . . . (me that is). The Knight rifle, solid as a rock itself, rested on the boulder, ready to do the deed. When the boar turned broadside, I let the crosshairs settle in tight and squeezed the trigger. BOOM!

The Swift bullet, chugging along at 1,500 feet a second, thumped into the big boar, ending the adventure. Hunting grizzly bears with a muzzleloader, while undeniably rewarding, is an exercise in discipline. One mistake and, well, you just don't make a mistake or you might not be around to tell about it.

Understanding Bears

Grizzly bear, Wyoming.

One could go on for pages and pages, talking about North America's bears and their varying and interesting lifestyles, but we'll try to summarize here in a few paragraphs.

The grizzly bear and Alaska brown bear are different versions of the same species, *Ursus arctos*. The prominent humps on their shoulders, and long claws, distinguish these bears from black bears. (But color alone doesn't always work as a distinguishing point, because many black bears aren't black at all.)

Grizzlies grow 6 to 8 feet long and weigh 500 to 800 pounds, though a few big fellows might weigh even more. Brown bears are huge, with some big boars weighing 800 to 1,200 pounds, and a few getting even bigger than that.

Grizzlies and brown bears eat what they want! True omnivores, they'll forage for berries, roots, grasses … or hunt elk, moose, sheep, deer, even livestock (which gets grizzlies into scuffles with the ranching community). They'll dig up marmots, ground squirrels and other burrowing animals too. Of course, the brown bears are famous for their love of salmon when the fish are making their spawning runs.

A black bear might be black, brown, cinnamon-colored or even blond, depending on where you find him, and that could be anywhere across Alaska and Canada and the northern states, as well as the coastal Northwest U.S. and the Rockies. The non-black bears seem primarily to inhabit the far western reaches of this range. An adult boar will weigh 200 to 400 pounds or maybe even more, depending on his age and how much forage is available. A sow will weigh 150 to 200 pounds.

Black bears are omnivores too, eating any and all variety of berries, nuts, fruits, crops, fish, small mammals they hunt, and carrion.

All bears smell and hear well. Their vision is good too, but not quite as extraordinary as their smelling and hearing. They are wary and elusive, and are hard to find in the wilderness habitats they call home.

Cinnamon-colored black bear, Alberta.

It's work. Good work mind you, but work nonetheless. The "big bears" all demand discipline. Whether the hunter is pursuing grizzlies in the mountains as I was, polar bears from a dogsled in the high arctic or brown bears on Kodiak Island, a hunter must maintain strict control over his actions.

While a big black bear can square out at seven feet, one of the big bears will square out at over nine feet; 11 feet for the largest brown and polar bears. A black bear might weigh in at 500 pounds for a monster, but a monster brown bear will push 1,500 pounds. Skull size for a big black bear might be 20 inches Boone and Crockett (width of the skull added to the length of the skull) while a polar or brown bear can measure more than 30 inches!

HUNTING "KILLER BEARS": THE DANGER IS REAL

"Bear kills two people at Liard Hotsprings." "Man killed saving kid from bear." "Children watch bear kill mom." "Man survives grizzly attack." "Animal problems, bears, cougars moving into urban areas." "Maulings shock community." "B.C. man hailed as hero in fatal bid to save others from attack by bear." "Bothersome bears cause uproar."

Lead-ins for some grotesque Hollywood movie? Some type of sick joke? Flashbacks from someone's worst nightmare?

Sadly not. The headlines are real. They are headlines that have become all too common in the newspapers the last few years. More specifically they are the tragic result of an increasing number of bear/human encounters.

Stories that require such violent headlines were formerly quite rare everywhere in North America.

But of late they are becoming frighteningly regular, especially in the beautiful mountainous regions of our continent. And it isn't just outdoors people, hunters, fishermen and the like who are the victims of the headlines. The "Killer Bears" have become so dangerous that even gentle tourists are being terrorized.

A case in point is the sad story of Patti McConnell, 37, of Paris, Texas. She was totally innocent, totally unaware that quiet summer a few years ago, of the dangers associated with visiting the bear-infested province of British Columbia. Had she been aware, she certainly would not have been walking with her two children, son Kelly, 13, and daughter Kristen, 7, along a well-used boardwalk that led to a well-known tourist destination, the Liard Hotsprings.

The 220-pound predatory male black bear attacked Patti's son, Kelly, and she did as any mother would, she tried to save her child. By all accounts, her heroic actions did save Kelly from the worst of the mauling. Patti, however was not saved. She died of her injuries. As did another hero in the horrifying ordeal, Ray Kitchen, 57. Ray heard Patti's screams and came running to the rescue. The big bruin, jaws already dripping, tore into its new victim, killing him. Eventually that bear, still standing over his prey, fell

Heed any and every warning you get, whether verbal or written, when entering bear country. Your life could depend on it.

before a hail of lead from the gun of another good Samaritan, but not before two humans were dead and two mauled.

The questions abound. Why did this tragic event happen in today's world? How indeed when the science exists to control and manage wildlife, even potentially dangerous animals like bears? The answer may lie in the actions of the governments

Don't push your luck! He knows you're there.

ern British Columbia for a little camping and hunting. Fumerton and Caspell left Shane's wife and child in camp on one recent October with a promise that they would return at dark. They did not return.

Four days later, their partially eaten bodies were recovered from the site of a grizzly attack. Located by helicopter first, the bodies of the two young outdoorsmen could not be retrieved until two out of the three aggressive grizzlies, standing over the bodies, were destroyed. There were no survivors to tell the tale of what transpired that fateful day in October of 1995 when the grizzlies claimed the lives and bodies of Shane and William.

Would those men be alive today if the grizzly bear season had been extended instead of curtailed during the years previous? Maybe. Maybe not. The answer will never be known, but what is known is that all bear encounters are increasing in the province, and the bears are getting more brazen as the following story will attest.

In a bizarre example of grizzly behavior, even by "Killer Bear" standards, a bear attacked two men while they sat in their airplane! John Hodgson and his friend Harvey Hurtubise were loading their gear onto their small floatplane when a grizzly charged. The bear jumped onto one of the floats and hit the side of the plane. One paw full of claws pounded right through the side of the plane while the other went inside the doorway. When the bear's forward momentum stopped, the bear's fangs were only 12 inches from Hodgson. Thwarted, the bear eventually gave up and left.

In another, less bizarre but far more frightening fall grizzly bear attack that occurred a week or so after the attack on the airplane, another grizzly mauled six campers. The actual cause of the attack originated in British Columbia a full year before the attack. That year, the British Columbia town of

of the day. Instead of reacting to the increasing incidence of bear attacks in the obvious way—increasing the hunting seasons for bears—many governments have actually decreased bear hunting opportunities during the last five years!

Had the government responsible acted properly, instead of bending to the will of vocal minorities calling for a moratorium on bear hunting, two more young men, killed by a grizzly bear, might still be alive today. Shane Fumerton, 32, his wife of one year, their infant son and a friend, William Caspell, 40, headed into the mountains of south-

Revelstoke had a problem grizzly bear that had become habituated to the town landfill site. Though the conservation officers were only following government policy and could not know it at the time, the problem grizzly they captured and relocated rather than destroyed, was destined to become infamous.

When that bear wandered into the campground near Lake Louise, Alberta, she was starving: starving enough to begin pulling six screaming campers from their tents. By some miracle, all were alive when the attack was over.

The nightmares brought on by "Killer Bears" are far too numerous to mention. Nearly everyone who spends time in the wild outdoors has a story to tell of narrowly escaping from a bear. Few, however, come as close to *never* telling their story as Dale Graham. He was making his way through the forest when he was attacked by a grizzly. Point-blank range does not adequately describe how close the grizzly was when Graham pulled the trigger of his rifle. The bear was tearing at the flesh on Graham's leg at the time. The grizzly dropped him and Graham headed back to his truck. He made it and was weaving down the road, in shock, when he was discovered by two other hunters.

Unbelievably, Bob Nichol's experience was even more dramatic. Nichol was stalked and attacked by a grizzly very near the date Graham was attacked. Nichol didn't have a chance to react before the first blow struck him in the chest and knocked him down. As the bear held the hunter down with its feet and began trying to pull chunks of flesh from his legs, Nichol attempted to reach for his rifle. His attempts to reach the rifle were futile. The bear would lunge for his throat every time he tried. In less time than it takes to tell it, the grizzly worked its way up the hunter's body, tearing at his groin, stomach and chest on the way up toward Nichol's head. Determined not to die that way, Nichols worked his arm free and pulled out his knife. He stabbed at the bear again and again, eventually severing the bear's jugular vein and in so doing, killing his own would-be killer.

Grizzly bears are not solely responsible for the continuing carnage across North America. Black bears, like the one that killed the two heroic people at the beginning of this section, also claim "Killer Bear" status.

CONCLUSION

As you can see by these stories, bears of all kinds can be mean, protective, aggressive, surly ... and downright murderous. It's not their fault—they are just being bears.

But that's what makes bear hunting exciting, to be sure. Whether you're sitting over a bait pile in Minnesota, following a pack of hounds in West Virginia or stalking a tidal flat in Alaska, you're hunting game that can hunt back. And that makes bear hunting one of the most exciting hunting adventures you can ever experience.

A big black bear with his claim. Your best bet is to leave him alone, because he's most certainly in an aggressive and protective mood.

Equipment for Bear: Rifles, Loads, Bullets & Optics

Bigger is better. The more "OOMMFF!" a rifle has, the better it is for taking bears consistently and effectively. As an outfitter for more than 1,000 bear hunts, I've had more experience with downed bears than all but a very, very few others. Speaking from that experience, the more foot-pounds of energy a rifle packs, the less the odds that I'll have to crawl around some hellhole looking for an enraged bear. To avoid this, I recommend my hunters bring rifles of .300 Winchester Magnum or larger. As a backup gun, I use a custom-made, ultra-light .300 Weatherby Magnum with a titanium action. It's a bolt action; bolt-action rifles are the most reliable and really the only choice for the serious bear hunter.

One of the best all-around rifles for bear is the .338 Winchester Magnum. Properly loaded, it will perform magnificently on all the bear species. For the bigger bears, rifles in the league of the venerable .375 Holland and Holland should be considered, if you can take the recoil. Again—speaking personally and as an outfitter and guide—I abhor muzzle brakes. They allow almost anyone to handle the substantial recoil of these big guns, but they blow the ears out of the guide. If you must, order your big gun with a detachable muzzle brake. Blow your own ears out at the range, but then unscrew the muzzle brake for the hunt.

Hunters sitting over bait, waiting for black bears, can get away with smaller rifles because the shots

Both an arrow (left) and a bullet (right) can put a bear down for good. Arrows must be razor sharp—and that's that; a huge draw weight isn't that big of a deal. For your rifle, use a caliber of .300 Winchester or larger for the grizzlies and browns. You could get by with something as light as a .270 for black bears over bait. Muzzloader hunters will want 100 grains of powder pushing a 300-grain projectile.

are generally closer and the hunter safer. A .270 is adequate when the shot is close and the problem variables—such as wind, distance and shot angle—are "controlled" by virtue of the hunting method. On a baited hunt, the hunter generally has a rest, isn't breathing hard and has plenty of time to aim, so the larger rifles, while still better, are not absolutely necessary.

For those who must use muzzleloaders for their bear, I suggest the following as the minimum: a .50 caliber loaded with l00 grains of powder, shooting a 300-grain bullet, preferably one that is saboted down to .45 caliber (not .44).

Which brings us around to bullet size and construction. For backup, I use 200-grain Federal Trophy-bonded bullets. A heavy bullet is better than a light bullet and a well-constructed "premium" bullet is better than a bullet designed to be used for anything from coyotes to moose. Our hunters have had the best success with Swift A-Frame bullets, Federal Trophy-bonded bullets and the copper bullets such as Fail-Safe. Muzzleloader hunters would do well to load up with the 300-

grain Swift A-Frame bullet and archers should use chisel-tipped broadheads with razor blade inserts.

For those archers in the crowd, draw weight is nowhere near as important as arrow placement. A bow of 50-pound pull is adequate if the arrow is razor sharp and placed properly.

All that said, without proper bullet or arrow placement, it "don't matter a hoot" how powerful the gun behind the bullet is, or how sharp the broadhead is.

Aim for the lungs. Lungs are where to aim. Lungs, lungs and lungs. You get the point. A bear shot through both lungs is a dead bear, a found bear and a safe bear. The lung shot goes for rifle hunters, muzzleloader hunters and archers. Wait for the bear to turn broadside and aim to hit the bear one-third of the way up the body, directly above the armpit. Simple, right? Unfortunately not. That's why a big gun is better.

When that big bear of a lifetime walks out in front of you, the last thing you need is a fogged scope. I use Leupold scopes exclusively because we've never had a Leupold product quit on a hunter during one of our hunts. They are *the only* scope manufacturer I can say this of. The variable power scopes of 2 to 7 or 3 to 9 power are both durable and practical for the serious bear hunter. A 40mm objective is more than adequate as far as light gathering goes.

The yellow crosshair marks where you should aim with rifle or bow: lungs, lungs, lungs. Nothing fancy, just shoot him in the lungs.

Chapter 8

MOOSE: WORKING HARD FOR OUR BIGGEST DEER

BY JUDD COONEY

I spotted the humongous bull's antlers flashing in the morning sun as he moved through a dense willow and alder thicket, about the same time I heard his resonant grunting drifting on the still morning air. I watched awestruck as the bull crashed out of the dense brush, stalked menacingly to the edge of the lake, and stopped.

"Dang!" I muttered to my compadre, visualizing numerous turkey gobblers hung up on creeks, streams and swamps. "We're going to have to get around this lake and seduce that bull from his side of the lake," I declared knowingly to my hunting partner. HAH! A few seconds later it became obvious that I didn't know much about rutting moose, as the horny bull waded into the frigid water and was shortly swimming our way with only his massive antlers and head out of the water.

About the time the bull reached solid footing on our side of the lake, a second bull nearly the equal of the first appeared out of the brush and took to the water as well.

My partner George Fotiu and I both had Alberta moose tags. I figured there was a chance we might just arrow both bulls on this fine fall morning.

The first bull did not hesitate as I teased it up the timbered slope with a series of plaintive "hot-wired" cow moans. When the bull stopped at 15 yards I came to full draw and waited for the perfect shot. Unfortunately the bull sensed something amiss, finding camoed blobs instead of an amorous cow, and he turned to circle and pick up the wind. My arrow found its mark and sent the bull charging blindly back down the slope on his

Moose are big, but they are smart and wary, and they know how to get back into the brush and hide. They are tough to hunt!

final run. The second bull had followed in the first bull's footsteps, but when the arrowed moose came barreling down the hill in a wild charge, the second bull took off like a turpentined cat and disappeared around another timbered slope adjacent to the lake, never to return. George and I watched in silent reverence as the fatally arrowed bull lost momentum and sank silently onto the spongy moss.

You don't get the full impact of just how immense a bull moose is until you walk up to

Author Judd Cooney with a nice bull. You know you've shot something when you walk up to an animal that's this big.

a downed animal that weighs more than 1,600 pounds and stands 7 feet at the shoulder with antlers spreading more than 5 feet from tip to tip. At that time my moose was the largest moose taken with a bow in Alberta and sported a 61-inch spread. Talk about your immovable object! Fortunately in this case our guide, George and I were able to chainsaw our way through a minimum amount of downed timber and drive a 4X4 4-wheeler right to the moose. But that is not always the case, to be sure.

Generally moose hunting is *not* a do-it-yourself type of hunt. All nonresident Canada moose hunters are required to hunt with a licensed outfitter. Alaska moose hunting can be done on your own with the proper planning and execution of the hunt. But if you're a first-time moose hunter you'd be well-advised to hire the services of a professional outfitter. The state of Alaska requires a short, moose-oriented education course before they'll let you venture into the wilds on your own.

In the Lower 48, solo moose hunting is more feasible *if* you can get a license. All Shiras (Western or Mountain) moose permits are issued on a drawing basis, except the few that are designated to be sold to the highest bidder, or on a raffle by each of the states to add funds specifically to support their moose management programs.

HOW TO HUNT OUR LARGEST DEER

At first glance, moose hunting may seem easy: The animal is so big, it must be a cinch to find one and shoot him! Not true.

Moose are smart, with great eyes and ears. While it's true there are times when they are more vulnerable (e.g., the rut), it's also true that if you don't hunt hard and smart, you're not going to shoot a moose.

So here are some strategies and techniques for hunting our largest deer.

Hunting the Rut

The epitome of moose hunting has to be when the moose are in full rut and the bulls are susceptible to calling. Imitating the moaning pleas of a

Imitate the moaning pleas of a cow to pull in an amorous bull moose. The old birchbark megaphone, teamed with the human voice, still makes an effective call.

cow in heat, or getting a distant response and listening—with building anticipation and rising adrenaline level—to the grunts of an approaching bull is what moose hunting is all about.

Generally, in northern moose areas, the peak of the rut comes in the last two weeks of September. At this time the lusty bulls are roaming the country looking for cows in estrus and defending their territories against interlopers.

The best moose call is still the birchbark or plastic megaphone, coupled with the human voice, for imitating both the plaintive cow moans and the short grunts of the rutting bull. For such a huge animal, the noise moose make is rather subdued. But what it lacks in volume it makes up for in low frequency resonance which carries for considerable distances in moose cover.

When bulls spar or get serious about fighting, the racket they make is commensurate with their size and would be impossible to duplicate even if you could manage a set of 70-pound rattling antlers.

When a couple rutting bulls get serious about fighting, get ready for a real battle! These two are just sparring a little and testing the waters.

Some Canadian moose guides clack the dried scapula bones of a moose or cow together to imitate bulls sparring and pique the curiosity of any rival bulls within hearing range. Combining the rattling and clacking with cow moans and bull grunts can produce spectacular results during the rut.

Another guide technique is to imitate the urinating of a hot cow before breeding by splashing water with a foot, branch or canoe paddle, or by pouring water out of the call megaphone or a bucket. Rutting moose are not quiet and sedate little animals; they are huge, they are ready to do some breeding, and a lot of racket might just trip their switch.

Spot & Stalk Hunting

Spotting and stalking is probably the most popular and effective method of moose hunting and can be done before, during and after the rut. Good binoculars and a spotting scope are essential for this type of hunting, especially if you are being particular and hunting a trophy-sized bull. This tactic works well where there's some terrain for you to get up on and spot from, so it's especially suited to the West and Shiras moose hunting.

Like other rutting big game animals, a bull moose throws a little caution to the wind when his female objects of affection are in heat. That's when he's vulnerable.

Understanding Moose

Shiras moose, Wyoming.

Moose are the largest members of the deer family roaming the North American continent. There are three subspecies of moose to choose from.

The Shiras moose is the smallest member of the clan, with a big bull weighing 1,000 pounds or a little more and carrying antlers with a 50-inch spread. It is interesting indeed to see a moose up in the mountains. But like his cousins to the north and east, a Shiras moose is never far from water or wet areas. Look for willows. The Shiras moose is being well managed and is actually on the increase in the western states of Utah, Colorado, Montana, Wyoming and Idaho. These states issue a very limited number of nonresident licenses each fall on a drawing basis.

The Canada moose inhabits the woods, mountains, swamps and lake country of that country and a few of the northern states bordering Canada, such as Minnesota, Michigan, Maine and Vermont. The Canada moose is the second largest of the species,

Canada moose, Maine.

with a big bull topping the scales at 1,400 to 1,500 pounds and sporting antlers in the 60-inch range. These moose are most often associated with low-lands and conifer forests. The largest Canada bulls are taken in the northern reaches of British Columbia and Alberta, where the border between their range and the range of the somewhat larger Alaska-Yukon subspecies is only an imaginary line drawn on the maps. There are a very limited number of licenses issued for Canada moose and these are generally limited to residents only. Canada requires all nonresident aliens (U.S. hunters) to hunt with a licensed outfitter for moose.

The Alaska-Yukon moose is the largest of the subspecies. A big bull may weigh 1,800 pounds and carry antlers with a 72-inch or greater spread! These moose are often associated with low, wet brushland; river corridors make prime habitat.

Licenses for Alaska moose are available across the counter and the services of a licensed guide or out-fitter are not required to hunt these behemoths. But if you're hunting moose in the early season you'd better give serious thought to how you are going to get 1,000-plus pounds of meat and antlers out of the bush without losing the meat to spoilage. Waste like that is bad enough, but Alaska has very stringent and strictly enforced laws on wasting or losing game meat as well.

No matter what type of moose you pursue, they are interesting looking packages indeed. Long legs give them the ability to move through deep snow (some animals stand 7 feet tall at the shoulder). A dewlap hangs from the bull's chin. They are big animals, but they have good ears and noses, and moose will disappear into cover surprisingly fast when you make a hunting blunder.

Alaska moose on the tundra.

Spotting moose (left) is hard work. Moose country is huge, and though the animals are big, the immensity of the country swallows them up. Plus, moose are not afraid to set up shop in incredibly thick cover (right) that makes them even more difficult to locate.

Spotting the animal before it has a chance to spot you definitely gives you the advantage, and you need all you can get with these critters. Moose not only have the largest nose of any North American game animal, but it is also the most sensitive when it comes to picking up the scent of danger. My advice is to carry a small squeeze bottle filled with talcum powder so you can keep the wind currents working for you instead of against you. By constantly monitoring the wind when you are stalking or calling, you can maintain a position downwind of your quarry and increase your chances of success immeasurably. *Do not* take a moose's smelling ability lightly.

There is no way to combat swirling or erratic wind currents, and in such cases patience in waiting for another time is the only sensible tactic. If only I'd listened to my own advice on several unsuccessful attempts when I simply had to push the envelope! Many hunters don't give moose much credit in the smarts department, but my experience has shown a mature moose to be a canny adversary that can disappear into the almost impenetrable cover they frequent with the ease and subtlety of a wisp of fog—and just as silently.

A moose's hearing is on par with his sense of smell and the slight rustle or scrape of a foreign sound will get his full attention in short order.

A moose's eyesight is his biggest weakness. A still, camouflaged hunter is liable to get stepped on by an ardent moose intent on finding the love of his life. The fact that an adult moose's eyes are situated seven or eight feet above the ground does offset this factor a bit and calls for slow, painstaking stalking in all but the densest of cover.

Moose have a phenomenal ability to cover rough or inhospitable terrain such as bogs, sloughs and muskeg with ease. A meandering, browsing moose can easily outdistance a hunter trying to stay up with him. If you glass a feeding or moving moose, you had better plan your stalk to give you plenty of leeway for an intercepting course or you're going to get left behind. Moose legs are long, and the animals get from here to there quickly.

I once spotted a feeding bull along an alder-choked stream north of Alaska's Brooks Range and stayed within 75 yards of him for two hours, unable to get closer because his height gave him such a commanding view of the low willows he was feeding through. When he finally decided to move up the creek I tried to follow him. Every time he would disappear into a dense stand of alder/willow I would run like hell to catch up, and when he emerged on the far side I was the same distance from him. After a mile of this inane activity I realized he was too far from camp to even shoot and I was the one that was about dead from exhaustion while he strolled nonchalantly on his way, never realizing he was in any danger.

Moose have long legs and can move fast, covering a lot of ground when they seem to be just ambling along. Act now to intercept a moving moose.

Think Before You Shoot, Then Drop 'em Quick

I learned a valuable lesson on my first Alaska moose hunt many years ago when I was invited to accompany a pilot friend on a hunt to the Kenai Peninsula. The gun hunter was strictly meat hunting, and after locating a medium-sized bull on a hillside above a small lake where he could land the plane, he set the Cub down in another lake a mile away, and we moved in for the kill. You could still fly and hunt the same day back then, a practice that is illegal now.

Think for a moment before you pull the trigger or release the arrow. Every moose is a big package. Will you be able to get the meat and antlers out of the places where he will potentially drop?

When we got within 100 yards of the feeding bull, my companion touched off his new .338 Win. Mag. and fully expected the bull to take a nosedive into the alders. The bull showed no indication of even being hit! It took off down the hillside, plowing through the dense brush and alders like a runaway freight train headed for the lake. My partner was alternating his shots with some hearty cuss words while I, in my naivete, enjoyed the action. I should have been shooting.

When the moose finally expired, it was partially submerged in four feet of water and I soon found out what all the cussing was about. Butchering an immovable, 1,600-pound critter in waist-deep, icy-cold water is about on the same enjoyment level as having your hemorrhoids treated with a wire brush and Tabasco sauce. The only saving grace to this venture was the fact my pilot friend could taxi his Super Cub right up to the moose carcass. On my first moose venture I gained a lot of respect for the immensity of even a medium-sized bull moose, and the work involved in moose hunting.

Preparing for a float into moose country.

Float Hunting

Floating creeks, rivers and lakes in prime moose country, and combining calling with spot-and-stalk hunting, is probably one of the most enjoyable and painless ways of hunting moose, as long as your victim doesn't expire in the middle of the river or out in a lake or bog. Think about where he is before you pull a trigger or release an arrow!

During the fall, the scenery along the waterways in moose country is fantastic and the peace and tranquility has to be experienced to be fully appreciated. I guess if I had to pick my favorite method of moose hunting this would be it, and I've *never* killed a moose on a float trip hunting in Alaska or Canada.

TAKE THE MOOSE CHALLENGE

There are times when moose hunting can be the most exciting, challenging and gratifying hunt of a lifetime; however, moose hunting can also be so exasperating and frustrating you'll wish you had taken up golf or bowling instead. One thing you can bet on: Hunting moose is never boring and might even be addictive, so proceed with caution!

Rifles, Bows & Equipment for Moose Hunting

There have probably been more moose taken with the trusty old .30-30 than any other single caliber, and I've met a number of Native American hunters who have kept their families supplied with moose meat for years with nothing bigger than a .25-20. Bullet placement is far more important in making a clean kill on a bull moose than muzzle energy alone. An extra thousand pounds of muzzle energy sailing out the far side of a bull or parting the air over or under his chest isn't going to accomplish much, so practice, practice, practice with whatever gun you plan on using for your moose hunt.

I've seen a big bull absorb three chest hits from a .375 H&H Mag. pushing 250-grain bullets and still cover 400 yards before collapsing. I've also watched a bull drop in his tracks from a single 140-grain .270 slug in the same place.

Be prepared for what happens after the shot. You get your moose out of the bush any way you can—here, by floating!

Size alone can make a badly hit moose an exceedingly tough adversary, and you can bet when they get to choose their final resting place it darn sure won't be in your best interest (see sidebar on page 131). Regardless of the caliber rifle or muzzleloader you choose for your moose hunting venture, master its every idiosyncrasy and learn to shoot it accurately at all hunting ranges and under a variety of hunting conditions.

Big moose are my kind of bowhunting animal! I've taken Canada and Alaska moose with bow and arrow and plan on a Shiras hunt in the near future. Moose can be taken with a longbow, recurve or compound in the 60-pound-pull range as long it is pushing an arrow with a razor-sharp broadhead.

He's big, that's for sure. But the most important aspect of your shooting is not the size of your rifle caliber or draw weight of your bow: It's hitting him cleanly and solidly in the boiler room, the lung region (yellow crosshairs). If you're using a bow, don't hit that shoulder blade!

My first Alaska bull that had a 64-inch spread and placed well up in the Pope & Young record book was taken with an 85-pound compound, Easton XX75 aluminum arrows and 125-grain Phantom broadheads. I stalked to within 15 yards of the bedded bull, and when he stood up quartering away, I put my arrow in behind the last rib. The heavy arrow penetrated through the chest and buried in the offside shoulder. The bull made it 40 yards before collapsing in the only gully within miles. It took my partner and me four hours to quarter the bull and then get the meat to a small stream 100 yards away. We ended up floating the load of meat a mile down the stream on 10 x 50 truck inner tubes with alder branches laced across them to support the meat. This method turned a meat packing job into a miserable one, and my companion vowed never to hunt moose again. Kind of similar to my first moose adventure!

Any rugged, one-piece or replaceable-blade broadhead such as the Phantom, Thunderhead 125 or Zwickey is capable of producing a clean, quick kill on a moose when properly placed. I do not recommend retractable or "flip-open" blade broadheads for an animal the size and toughness of a moose. Often the secondary cutting of an imbedded broadhead can be the determining factor in the success or failure of your moose hunt, and "flip-open" broadheads are sadly lacking in this department as are several others, in this author's opinion.

Beyond that, the story on optics is the same as for any other big game: Get the best binoculars you can--clear and bright in 7 or 8 power—and use a spotting scope (a good 20 power is fine) if you're worried about analyzing inches of antler before you shoot.

If you're doing it yourself, make plenty of provisions for dressing, skinning, cutting up and transporting that moose, because you aren't going to be dragging him. The other option, as the old joke in the West goes, is:

Question: "What's the best moose to shoot?" Answer: "The one bringing his fourth hoof onto the road!"

Chapter 9

CARIBOU: A HUNT IN THE WILD

By Wayne van Zwoll

The last day of a hunt brings pressure, even more so on this hunt because I had committed to using a muzzleloader. Iron sights and a patched round ball mandate close shots; on the treeless tundra, those come hard.

I'd seen a handful of big caribou bulls and was on my fourth sneak when a palmated antler suddenly popped up over the horizon. Because the bull's head was still behind the hill, I chanced a dash across a swampy meadow, then bellied onto the slope and inched my way up.

The antler appeared again as I crawled forward to a hummock, capped the nipple and brought the hammer back. The bull stepped over the ridge 25 yards away and immediately saw me. But I'd already set the trigger on the .56 caliber T/C Renegade. The caribou wheeled at the blast, staggered away behind the blue smoke, and dropped.

A GRAND HUNT IN GRAND SURROUNDINGS

Caribou look too bovine to be exciting. But my caribou hunts have all been memorable. That's partly because caribou country is truly wild. You hunt animals that may not have been hunted before, where real caribou trails are the thoroughfares. The North also brings you in touch with Inuits, the hardy people that for centuries have hunted whales, seals, polar bears and caribou above "the land of little sticks." Camping with Inuits is a lesson in resourcefulness.

Author Wayne van Zwoll with a muzzleloader bull caribou.

Generally, where there's one caribou, there are many more ... if they are there yet at all!

Another thing about caribou that draws you back is their visibility. The chalk-maned bulls stand out like ivory chess pieces against the dark green lichen and gray slab-rock of the Arctic. In late August, their huge antlers blink bright red in the sun as velvet peels in shreds.

You hunt caribou then—before sleet and snow come and before, far to the south, the leaves turn color. Hunting bare-antlered caribou in mid-September means hunting hard against the teeth of winter. Winds of 40 mph and horizontal sleet can make caribou country feel like winter, even before Labor Day.

In August you'll hunt in light woolens, while the bog grasses turn yellow and blueberry leaves turn scarlet. The white-socks, blackflies and mosquitoes are on the wane. You may hop in a broadbeamed Inuit freighter canoe, the 20-horse outboard pushing you along endless chains of lakes, up rapids that feed pools alive with brook trout and arctic char. You'll glass the shorelines and the hills behind, but sometimes you'll see caribou swimming. They ride low in the water, their big feet driving their antlers like rafts of fallen trees cutting a wake for tiny tails carried upright.

You might think you're in the back pasture looking at a cow path when you see a caribou migration trail. Of course, the only caribou trail that really matters is the one with caribou traveling it.

Packing for a Caribou Hunt

Not all caribou hunts bring you such adventure as my first, but the far north is unforgiving country, and you're smart to prepare for a blast of harsh weather. Here's what I pack for caribou hunts by boat.

CLOTHES

1 pair lightweight, waterproof hiking boots or pacs (or knee-high rubber boots)

1 pair camp moccasins or athletic shoes

1 set long underwear

1 pair wool pants, with heavy leather belt

1 wool shirt

1 pair lightweight cotton pants and sweatshirt

2 pairs heavy wool mitts with flop-open finger ends for trigger access

1 wool hat

1 heavy wool jacket

1 set rain gear—either "commercial fisherman" rubber or high quality Gore-Tex

You often need to go by plane to get into good caribou country. Once there, you might then travel by boat to get in to the animals.

HUNTING KIT

❏ flashlight and extra batteries

❏ compass

❏ canteen

❏ 2 safety flares

❏ signal mirror

❏ whistle

❏ snack food

❏ folding knife with 4-inch lock-back blade

If you're after barren ground caribou you'll likely be in Alaska or the Yukon or the Northwest Territories on a home range as broad as the lower 48 states. Most Quebec-Labrador caribou inhabit the treeless northern half of Quebec, a province three times the size of France. To the east, Newfoundland holds the big-boned, small-antlered woodland caribou in timbered swamps. The less common mountain caribou lives near treeline in northern British Columbia and the Yukon. Most hunters start their caribou affairs with the barren ground or Quebec-Labrador variety. I did.

FIRST CARIBOU HUNT

It was years ago, on the tundra above Hudson Bay. We loaded the freighter canoes in the small Inuit community of Repulse Bay, where I watched

A caribou hunting base camp.

Traveling in big freighter canoes and being guided by natives adds to the caribou hunting mystique.

Icy Greeting

We awoke the third morning to find garage-size chunks of ice piled against the shore, blocking our view of the bay. I climbed one and was stunned to see nothing but mountains of ice to the south and west. There was no open water in sight! We broke camp anyway, the Inuits maneuvering their beached canoes into tiny channels of water. Engines were out of the question. We poled a few feet, bracing oars against ice. Then an Inuit jumped to a floater, grabbed a towline and heaved the bow onto the ice.

Next, passengers scrambled out and dragged the canoe forward until the bow found water, hoping the narrow channels wouldn't suddenly close, crumpling our canoes and a ton of gear between converging blocks of ice. One Inuit pulling a towline barely escaped a dunking as a floater spun under his weight, the black jaws of the bay gaping beneath him.

barefoot boys play with plastic boats in puddles iced over the night before. The villagers carved fat from a beached whale for their pantries and gave the meat to their sled dogs, kept on a treeless island nearby where they could roam free but not endanger infants. An old man beamed as he showed me a sealskin kayak he'd just finished—as sleek and seamless as the best modern fiberglass craft.

The steely black water of the bay danced white ahead of a gray wind. We motored perhaps 20 miles east, then set up a spartan tent camp near the shore. A couple of rainy days later I had killed a caribou. So had a 70-year-old Inuit who took six with an iron-sighted .22 rimfire and packed the heavy bundle of hides to camp with a rope looped across his shoulders. Then the wind swung around to the south.

Lunch in caribou country. It might be brook trout, seal, caribou tenderloins or char, as shown here.

Lessons in Survival

At mid-afternoon we called a halt. While a couple of men set up a Coleman stove, a sharp-eyed Inuit lad spied the head of a seal in a pocket of open water. Deftly he levered a round into an iron-sighted Marlin .30-30 and let drive. Almost before the "smack" of the bullet, our boy had shoved in the lightest canoe. There was no telling how much time you would have after a shot. Fat seals might float for a minute, but seals in poor flesh will sink almost instantly.

Gaffed and retrieved, the seal was immediately unzipped by the Inuits manning the stove. They put almost everything into a pot of boiling water—even the intestines, which they emptied first by stripping them between thumb and forefinger. I ate some intestine and found it salty but quite palatable. Meanwhile, a scouting party had climbed to a pinnacle of ice. They returned, conferred in the Inuit tongue with the elder and turned the canoes around.

We would have to go back or risk a night in the ice jam, where a storm could crush us. We reached the shore exhausted, slept till mid-morning—and awoke to a north wind that had pried the ice apart, leaving us room to motor out into the bay again.

IT ISN'T A SURE THING

Steve Ashton, who helps Inuit outfitters reach caribou hunters in the U.S., offers a tip for first-timers in the North: Expect to work for your

Understanding Caribou

No matter what type of caribou you'll be hunting (probably the barren ground version in central and western parts of caribou range, the Quebec-Labrador subspecies in the east), you'll be hunting a handsome animal that you'll often find in vast herds. Both types live on flat, open ground where the only plants are lichens, mosses and maybe some dwarf shrubs and conifers.

Bulls of these subspecies weigh anywhere from 175 to 350 pounds, and the antlers are, quite simply, spectacular on a mature animal. A bull's antlers might be 5 feet long! Cows grow much smaller antlers, which usually are at most a couple feet long and quite spindly.

Caribou migrations are famous—either for how spectacular they are (with thousands of animals streaming across the tundra) or for their absence during the week you happen to have booked your hunting trip! These migrations are, of course, to get the animals to winter range. The biggest herd bulls lead this fall migration, while the pregnant cows lead the reverse movement in spring. A herd might travel 30 miles in one day.

The peak of breeding occurs in mid- to late October, and herd bulls will stay very busy traveling back and forth through the cows, looking for ones in heat to breed.

Sparring bulls. That's a lot of antler to be clicking and clacking!

Sometimes you sit and wait, wait, wait for caribou ... and then you wait some more. As the author says, it isn't a sure thing!

caribou. The low cost of tundra caribou hunts compared to other wilderness adventures doesn't mean that caribou are pushovers. Sometimes you'll find them in abundance; sometimes you won't find them at all. As I write, I just returned from a camp on the migration route of the big Mulchatna

herd in Alaska. In two weeks I saw perhaps a dozen caribou, and no mature bulls. Just days earlier, the deeply rutted caribou trails in that unit had been alive with animals. "They swarmed over the hills like flies," said my guide. "But they're gone now." Indeed they were.

One Quebec pilot told me of looking in vain for caribou during a contract flight for government biologists. "I flew for hours where the caribou should have been moving and didn't see a thing. I was about to give up when I spotted a single bull. I homed in on him and found the tail of a herd. For the next 65 miles I was over the backs of caribou. How many? Gosh, I don't know. How many caribou can you fit in a herd 65 miles long?"

Outfitters dread concentrations like that. Hunters in one camp might be overrun with caribou, while other camps go without. One year some Inuit camps in Quebec produced so poorly that Steve Ashton shut those camps in mid-season. He phoned the hunters and told them to stay home.

If you're there when the caribou are moving, it's quite a spectacle, generating hunting excitement the likes of which you'll remember forever. These bulls are on the move and a lake is no barrier at all.

KEYS: MOVEMENT & MIGRATION

As Quebec has about a million caribou, the problem isn't animal numbers, but movements. The 30,000 animals taken each year in that province come from a vast territory—300,000 square miles of taiga and tundra. The biggest groups of animals cover a miniscule piece of that real estate, so being in the right place is important. For a long time, outfitters could predict where the caribou would be, based on records. Then the animals moved in ways and at times they had not before. No one has figured out why. Forage, weather and insects all affect caribou movement, but none of those factors seemed responsible.

"Radio tracking has shown that caribou stay near calving grounds until after the peak of calving the second week of June," says Steve Ashton. "By July the bugs are bad, and caribou bunch up to reduce their skin exposure." Black flies, nose bots and mosquitoes force the animals to seek relief near large bodies of water where they can catch cool breezes. Bugs do invisible damage by keeping the caribou from foraging. But bugs have always done that, and caribou have moved predictably.

Steve suspects El Niño weather for unexpected herd migrations another year. "We had a very warm September, and some caribou migrated 120 miles north before heading south to winter. Others traveled in circles, and some caribou didn't seem to move at all." (Not moving at all isn't good for caribou or hunters, because migration allows tundra plants to recover. After heavy grazing pressure, lichen, on which caribou depend, can take 40 years to regenerate.)

Mobility—big, long-range mobility—is often key if you want to shoot a caribou. Book with an outfitter who will transport you to some new territory if the animals aren't moving (or have already passed) through your hunt area.

Strong Populations

Quentin van Ginhoven, a contract biologist with Quebec's Department of Environment and Wildlife, tells me the provincial caribou population is booming—though keeping tabs on the footloose animals is costly and done only periodically. "By our count, the George River herd grew from about 5,000 animals in the 1950s to 800,000 recently. The Leaf River herd had 260,000 at that time." Calving in the George River herd occurs just southeast of where that river enters Ungava Bay. Leaf River caribou calve from the mouth of the Leaf northward on the Ungava Peninsula.

To track the herds, biologists collar females in summer, males in October after the antlers have hardened. Most animals are caught by net gun from helicopters or inflatable boats. Small VHS transmitters on collars emit continuous signals that last five to six years. The pulse changes if the animal doesn't move for several hours. The liability of VHS transmitters is their short range of 30 kilometers. To supplement them, biologists try to keep "Argos" collars on 15 animals in each caribou herd. The Argos transmitters tap into a pair of satellites that monitor environmental data and make 22 circumpolar trips per day. The Argos devices weigh a hefty 5 pounds apiece and last only two years even when transmitting at one-minute intervals just six hours every five days. But the signals can be picked up in offices far away, so there's a great savings in air time.

But knowing where caribou are doesn't put them within reach of hunters. To give their clients a better chance when caribou are elsewhere, the best outfitters increase their own mobility. Inuit camps operating under the banner of Arctic Adventures in Quebec share an Otter (airplane) so that hunters can fly to spike camps if they need to. The hunters tender a deposit for this service at the beginning of their hunt, but it's refunded if they don't have to fly to find caribou.

DON'T GIVE UP

Being in a camp after the caribou have left is like missing the last flight of the week at an airport. On the other hand, a day or two or three of poor hunting doesn't mean you'll go home empty. Twice I've filled out on the last day, and once I declined a fine bull with just hours to go. My favorite last-minute tale, though, is one of five

archers who hunted in vain for most of a week.

With only one caribou down and packed for a noon airlift on the final day, the disconsolate bowmen awoke at dawn to a splashing in the nearby lake shallows. One hunter peeked out of his tent to see a veritable fleet of caribou clogging the lake. More animals were pouring like ants off the far slope. On they came, right through camp, as the archers scrambled for their bows. They shot nine animals in two hours.

No, you mustn't expect fairy-tale endings *every* time.

JUDGING ANTLERS

When caribou are thick, you can afford to be selective. But picking the biggest set of antlers isn't always easy.

Caribou antlers comprise four main parts: the beam, the brow or shovel, the bez or second point, and the top. (There's a rear point to consider too, but it doesn't affect antler score as much as the other components.) If you've not shot caribou before, every mature bull may look huge. Even cow antlers, tiny in comparison, are as large as most whitetail racks! During a caribou migration, you'll see forests of antlers marching across the tundra.

Don't give up! Be out there—waiting and looking or walking and looking. The tundra is a magical place to be anyway, and when the caribou start coming, you want to be there ready for action.

Caribou antlers come in all shapes and sizes. Pick out ones you think are beautiful for whatever reason— mass, lots of points, height, deep shovels, graceful and sweeping curves. The author offers plenty of advice on evaluating trophy potential, but adds an even more important note: "Antler scores remain an artificial and inadequate measure of a trophy." Take a caribou you like, and take home a symbol and memories of one of the last truly wild places on earth.

The thing to remember about caribou antlers is that they're all smaller than they look. You'll notice right away that they're all different and that very few excel in all aspects. A bull with double shovels may have weak tops; one with great width of beam may have spindly bez points. Unless you're after a bull for the record book, you needn't consider antler inches—better to pick a rack that you like aesthetically. Even the imperfect among them are beautiful; antler scores remain an artificial and inadequate measure of a trophy.

It's not a bad idea to leave your rifle slung on your shoulder the first day, if you're surrounded by caribou. Take that day just to look—bearing in mind, of course, that caribou are mobile and that arctic weather can change overnight. I've committed to more shopping over the years as I enjoy looking for something special. Sometimes a tag goes unfilled, but that's all right.

Waiting for the Right Thing

On a recent Quebec hunt, for instance, I wanted a heavy set of antlers with lots of palmation. I hunted without shooting for days while my campmates killed bulls.

Then, one afternoon, a group of bulls appeared on a distant hill. I hurried to intercept them and crawled to within 30 steps of a white-maned bull with great wide beams that also swept back to

form deep "Cs" in profile. His single shovel and nondescript tops saved him.

But while glassing him, I almost missed another bull with more compact antlers. In fact, the herd had fed away several hundred yards before I saw the bull's immense bez points and palmated tops. The shovel looked fine too.

I hurried after the animals, actually running between the startled youngsters at the group's rear, counting on surprise to get me one brief standing shot. Sure enough, when I had come within 150 yards of the bull, caribou scattering to his sides alarmed him. He turned to look at me as I dropped to a sit, the sling already in place. Two quick breaths, the crosshairs settled, and a 125-grain Nosler from my .260 Remington ended the hunt.

If you go back after caribou a second or third time, you might just find yourself passing up some caribou as you enjoy the country waiting for "the right thing." This isn't snobbery; it prolongs your hunting time in a wonderful, isolated land.

Caribou Contacts

Barren Ground Caribou

Barry Taylor
Arctic Safaris
Box 1294
Yellowknife, NWT
X1A 2N9 Canada

Mountain Caribou

Stuart Maitland
Eureka Peak Outfitters
POB 1332
100-Mile House, British Columbia
V0K 2E0 Canada

Quebec-Labrador Caribou

Steve Ashton
Arctic Adventures
19950 Clark Graham
Baie d'Urfe, Quebec
H9X 3R8 Canada

Woodland Caribou

Ron Parsons
Owl's Nest Lodge
POB 2430, Station C
St. John's, Newfoundland
A1C 6E7 Canada

More was the satisfaction because I'd shopped specifically for such a bull. It turned out to be the best in camp.

Of course, you won't always succeed in meeting high standards. On another hunt I insisted that my partner shoot a magnificent bull that was too far for a sure shot with my iron sights. I later passed up a very good caribou the last day. My friend had collected such a grand specimen that other bulls paled in comparison. Even the best of them didn't seem worth shooting.

You may call me a snob for being selective, but I just enjoy hunting caribou. I also enjoy eating them and have shot bulls with mediocre antlers late in the hunt. Because a hunter is allowed two caribou in many areas, you can afford to fill the larder quickly, take the self-inflicted pressure off, and look for those special antlers the rest of your trip.

You take home more than just meat and trophies from caribou country. If you're lucky enough to hunt with some native guides (above), you'll have plenty of memories—and stories to tell—of the once-in-a-lifetime kind. And, sooner or later on your hunt, you'll probably pick out and shoot a beautiful bull (left), one you'll be proud of for a long time.

OTHER REWARDS

The rewards of caribou hunting don't come only with a kill. On caribou hunts I've seen polar bears and black wolves. I've watched the northern lights splash and shimmer, heard the calls of emperor geese and felt the tug of 3-pound brook trout on light fly tackle. I've talked with Inuit people about life in the last truly roadless place in North America. I've eaten whale blubber, seal belly and grizzly bear steaks and have picked wild blueberries by the bucket. I've traveled by freighter canoe through the ice pack and have landed on mountain ridges in bush planes patched with electrician's tape.

So don't be fooled by that bovine look. Caribou hunting is more than just a walk in the pasture.

Rifles & Equipment for Caribou

Most any rifle will do in caribou country, as long as you can shoot straight out to 150 yards or so. Select good, tough, bright binoculars; and carry a spotting scope if you're concerned down to the precise inches of antler on the animal you're looking at.

Nor are powerful cartridges necessary. You can kill caribou handily with any deer round. Caribou are bigger than deer (a mature bull can weigh 400 pounds) but not exceptionally tough. A .243 is adequate, a .270 more than enough. Inuits commonly use smallbore centerfires (one chap I know hunts with a .17 Remington), but they are not trophy hunting and not limited to one week in the field. Their .22 rimfires work up close on young animals, which are curious and much easier to approach than old bulls. Even then, however, the .22 can be a crippler. One justification for using powerful cartridges locally is protection: caribou share the North with grizzly, brown and polar bears.

I prefer to walk for caribou, though on major waterways many hunters conduct all but the final stalk from a canoe, and on busy migration routes you'll do well waiting by a rock on a small rise.

Where weight and bulk don't matter, 10X50 binoculars from Leica or Swarovski will make long-term glassing easy on your eyes. On the march, I carry 8X30s or 10X42s. You'll need reach from your glasses, but not the big exit pupil (high light transmission) so important when you're probing shadowed timber for deer and elk.

Though you can see caribou far away, you seldom have to shoot far. So long-range rifles and big scopes aren't necessary. I shot my last bull in his bed at 80 yards with an iron-sighted .300 Savage. The sneak from half a mile away was the cream of the hunt.

Getting close enough to shoot a mature caribou with an arrow or round ball, you'd best wear camouflage, but check regulations; in some parts of caribou range, blaze orange is required. Caribou have good eyes. Sometimes you can fool them though, by crossing open spaces bent over like some four-legged animal.

Caribou seldom make the explosive exit characteristic of white-tailed deer. Instead, they veer away from suspicious objects and leave for distant horizons in a ground-eating shuffle. Because they are herd animals, you'll often have to contend with several sets of eyes. And don't forget their keen noses!

Chapter 10

SHEEP: A SPECIAL HUNTING ADDICTION

BY CHUCK ADAMS

I love hunting wild sheep—Dall, Stone, bighorns and desert rams. The best way I know to teach you about hunting them is to take you on a few hunts and talk about the animals and how I pursued them.

GETTING HOOKED

I first hunted North American wild sheep one August well over two decades ago. It might surprise some readers to know that I was packing a 7mm Remington Magnum on that trip—not the bow and arrow I've become well known for over the years. But sheep hunting is sheep hunting, no matter what weapon you use, and my first-ever outing embodied all that is good about these magnificent animals.

My friend Gaines Chesnut was the president of Redfield optical company at the time, and he invited me to help in the making of a Dall sheep film in Alaska. This "help" would consist of hunting hard, finding a trophy ram, and making a one-shot kill for the camera. I jumped at the

The author first got hooked on sheep while hunting and camping in the land of the Dall sheep.

opportunity. Who in their right mind would pass up a chance at American's most gorgeous and most prestigious big game animal?

That first sheep adventure opened my eyes to the world of hunting rams in remote, unspoiled habitat. During ten terrific days, we horsebacked into the wilds of eastern Alaska's Wrangell Mountains, camped in glacial valleys and climbed granite peaks. We spotted white sheep galore, including enough full-curl rams to keep our pulses

Opposite page (clockwise from top left): Rocky Mountain bighorn sheep, Dall sheep, Stone sheep and desert bighorn.

in overdrive. We never saw another man, another boot track or one clue to previous human habitation. Aside from state-of-the-art hunting and camera equipment, we might very well have stepped thousands of years backward in time.

Eight days later, as I squeezed the trigger and sent a 160-grain Sierra boattail bullet through my ram from 125 yards, I knew I was hooked on sheep hunting. All the stories I'd read by Grancel Fitz, Jack O'Connor and other great writers were certainly true. Sheep are special animals.

There are four varieties of wild sheep on our continent—Dall, Stone, Rocky Mountain bighorn and desert bighorn. All are similar in many respects, and quite different in others. They share a love for steep, remote terrain. They all possess incredibly keen eyesight. Their noses and ears are on a par with those of deer. They frequent open or semi-open habitat. All are stunningly beautiful, with continuously growing and thickening horns that reach full curl by age 8 or 10. All are a treat to hunt with rifle or bow.

I discovered notable differences between wild sheep during 16 idyllic months when I had the extreme good fortune to bowhunt and harvest all four varieties of North American sheep. This feat is called the Grand Slam, and it was something I had dreamed about doing ever since reading outdoor magazines as a kid. I went to my friendly banker, took out a loan, and booked four carefully researched hunts.

At last count, eleven archers and more than 1,000 gunners have taken Grand Slams on sheep. When I finished my own slam with an Arizona desert bighorn, it was the fourth recorded for a bowhunter. Take it from me … sheep hunting is special.

Dall Sheep

I knew from my Redfield rifle hunt that optics are essential for sheep—even starkly white Dall sheep in their gray-and-green above-timberline habitat. For my first-ever Dall sheep bowhunt, I selected a compact, one-pound 10X-30X Bushnell Stalker spotting scope and superb Zeiss 10X40 binoculars. I also purchased lightweight but

When hunting Dall sheep, you'll pack in—way in—and spend a lot of time behind the glass, looking.

durable backpack gear—Freighter Frame pack, Mountain House freeze-dried food, lightweight and waterproof hiking boots with neoprene soles, non-bulky clothes that let me dress in layers to accommodate fluctuating mountain temperatures, light rain gear, and a two-man North Face four-season tent rated for winds up to 110 mph.

My old friend and guide Duane Nelson had warned me we would cover dozens of miles on foot, spike-camping each night until we located rams. He also warned that his remote, 5,000-square-mile hunting area in the MacKenzie Mountains of western Northwest Territories produced unpredictable weather, even in late July. Daylight never completely faded during this earliest of all North American sheep hunts, but one 24-hour period could conceivably show you 80°F, bluebird skies best suited for a T-shirt, followed by 20° and snow flurries.

Our Dall hunt was typical of what you might expect in Alaska, the Yukon or the Northwest Territories. White-sheep hunting in all three places requires a bush-plane flight to a remote airstrip, lake or river. In our case, the landing point was northwestern Canada's huge, fast-flowing Keele River. Once our Twin Otter transport plane touched down and taxied to the dock, six other hunters and I unloaded duffels (limited to 100 pounds per person) and prepared to hunt in separate directions. Mine was a backpack hunt—the best way to reach unspoiled, untapped habitat. The other five hunters would cruise for sheep on horseback. This easier, more traditional method works well in places where sheep harvest is controlled, to ensure big rams in accessible spots.

In unregulated areas, like parts of Alaska, habitat accessible by horseback or ATV is usually hammered and devoid of trophy rams.

Duane and I were both accustomed to hard, physical hunting. We hiked 26 air miles during the next three days, scrambling over low stretches of stunted spruce and brush to reach higher, more open basins with lush grass and bubbling streams. All around, eroded teeth of ancient mountains gnawed at the clear northern sky.

In all types of sheep hunting, you must walk with your eyes as well as your feet. The first two hunting days, Duane and I moved and stopped, moved and stopped. We glassed every inch of visible terrain. Sheep tend to bed along rocky slopes and ledges, and feed on nearby patches of grass. Dall sheep are the easiest of all to see, but they still blend surprisingly well when tucked in shaded nooks and crannies.

You'll search and peer and walk and look for days on end, and then you'll find a whole band of Dall sheep.

Into the Rams

Not until hunt day number 3 did we spot a band of rams. Before the October rutting season, Dall females and lambs congregate thousands of feet lower than males. Rams hang in bachelor bands of 2 to 20, most often lounging along high peaks and hanging valleys. If there's grass, water and solitude, that's where the big boys are prone to be.

There were nine rams in that first band. Three were dandies, with full-curl horns jutting upward to the noseline or above. One was especially nice, with deep-sweeping curls and slightly flaring tips. Only an expert guide or long-time sheep hunter can judge horn length and mass with any degree of accuracy, but even I could count ten distinct annual growth rings on that largest ram's amber horns. I could also see how deeply his horns dropped compared to the other "tight curl" sheep in the bunch.

An average sheep dies of tooth failure at 11 or 12 years of age, and only reaches trophy size at 8 or 10. This ram was ripe for the taking.

The next four hours taught me more about sheep hunting than all the books and articles I had ever read. Those animals deliberately chose elevated vantage points, bedding and rising to feed periodically. But their very fiddle-footed nature finally worked to my advantage. All disappeared beyond a hogback. Duane and I hustled

Sheep Insights

Hunters who hear I've taken sheep with a bow are often open-mouthed with amazement. The general viewpoint seems to be that wild sheep are incredibly wary, and are usually shot from extreme distance.

I love wild sheep, but let me set the record straight.

Sheep seldom see people. They live in places where predators rarely congregate.

The author, Chuck Adams, with a beautiful Dall sheep ram.

They do not have the skittish, walking-on-eggshells personalities of white-tailed deer. With rare exceptions, a successful sheep hunter must be in fine physical shape to reach animals over rough, steep country. He must know how to use terrain and camouflage to hide from the eyes of rams. But he should not believe that sheep are larger than life. Compared to hard-hunted species like elk and mule deer, sheep often seem naive and incredibly calm.

The late, great Jack O'Connor was the Shooting Editor of *Outdoor Life* magazine for 40 years. More than anyone else, O'Connor put wild sheep "on the map" through his articles and books. He loved sheep, had several Grand Slams to his credit, and glamorized these animals as the ultimate in wild, thrilling targets.

Yet Jack O'Connor admitted that rams of any variety are most often shot at 150 yards or less. He also said that sheep require less skill to fool than some other American species.

O'Connor wrote on several occasions about rams that stood within rifle range as he field-dressed the animal he had shot. Find a modern whitetail or mule deer buck silly enough to do that!

This reality check on the true nature of sheep should take nothing away from your anticipation of the hunt. You will never work harder for a good animal, and you will be doing it in some of the most spectacular country in North America.

Here's a good Dall sheep ram. While these sheep's horns aren't incredibly massive, the animals are stunning nonetheless in their white coats.

STONE SHEEP

When I went after Stone sheep in my quest for the slam, I was so excited I could hardly strap myself into the Cessna 185 float plane. I knew I was embarking on the adventure of a lifetime.

My pilot flew south from Watson Lake into the fabled Stikine River Country of northern British Columbia, Canada. Stone sheep live only in British Columbia, and I was certain my guide Keith Holmes offered some of the very best big-ram hunting in that province. How did I know? I had done what every would-be sheep hunter should do. I had researched outfitters for many months beforehand, calling booking agents and clients to get a feel for what each professional had to offer. Keith made the cut.

From reading books and magazines, I already knew a bit about Stone sheep. Like Dall rams, Stones have relatively thin horns with bases 14 to $14^1/2$ inches around and fairly sharp, unbroomed tips in a majority of males. Unlike the two types of bighorn sheep I planned to bowhunt later on,

ahead, peeked beyond the ridge, and found all nine sheep bedded within 75 yards. The biggest was 53 yards away, broadside and placidly chewing his cud.

After double-checking the distance with my archery rangefinder, I drew my compound bow and sent an arrow through the 175-pound ram's lungs. His eight buddies gawked in confusion as he staggered downslope and pitched tail-over-teakettle. The remaining sheep ambled single-file up the steepest mountain in sight, looked back once, and disappeared forever.

Two Stone sheep rams. In general, you'll find Stone sheep in steeper, rougher, tougher country than you will Dall sheep.

You might have to fly in to Stone sheep country, and magnificent country it is.

Stone and Dall sheep both have a delicate facial appearance and horn mass to match. I knew Stone sheep were very similar to Dall sheep in body size and temperament but were less abundant and far more difficult to see.

Stone rams vary considerably in color, the same as German shorthaired hunting dogs. The lightest are salt-and-pepper gray, the darkest nearly solid brown or slate-gray. Some have "saddles" of dark color across more lightly mottled bodies. The classic, most desirable coloration is a dark-gray body with lighter neck and face.

I had heard and read that all color phases blended distressingly well with Stone sheep habitat. Those reports were definitely true.

Keith Holmes and I were old friends, and had hunted mountain goats several years before. We stuffed the normal complement of spartan backpack gear in his Super Cub float plane, flew a hundred miles deeper into his ultra-remote concession, and landed on a postage-stamp-sized lake only a Super Cub could navigate. Keith told me he'd seen a small band of rams five miles away on a previous hunt.

We erected his two-person dome tent on the shoreline, spent a night of half-sleep atop softball-sized rocks, and began climbing before dawn. A light frost covered the ground. Not one cloud cluttered the sky.

This country was different from Dall sheep habitat, with steeper slopes, more heavily wooded valleys, and smaller, more isolated clusters of peaks. Two hours and four miles later, we reached the lip of a dirty-gray basin some two or three miles across. Along the bottom were streaks of brilliant grass and a murky glacial creek.

"This is where the rams were last week," Keith confided.

The Glassing Game

We planted our butts and proceeded to glass. Like every other sheep guide I've known, Holmes carried 10X binoculars of top quality. In his pack was a Bausch & Lomb 15X-45X scope. This chunk of habitat fell away precipitously in all directions, so there was no walk-and-glass plan. We looked for sheep from one spot for nine straight hours—so long, in fact, that I was beginning to doubt the area.

The sun was dipping low when Keith grabbed my arm. "Two rams below that plateau to the south!" he hissed.

I looked intently, and finally saw the moving curve of one yellow-brown horn. Both sheep had been bedded in plain view, and both were up now and feeding. I was amazed how well they blended in at less than 800 yards.

Two rams turned into four and four turned into six. The half dozen animals appeared and disappeared like smoke, picking upward along a seemingly open hillside. One was noticeably larger than the rest. His left horntip rose well above the nose.

You'll do a lot of glassing on the prowl for Stone sheep.

A stalk for Stone sheep is often nothing short of adventure.

Moving In

The rams climbed with maddening slowness and finally vanished over the lip of the plateau. We trotted 600 yards, dodging boulders and sliding over unstable shale. The last 200 yards were sharply uphill, hand-over-hand across bare dirt and rock.

"Stop!" I whispered as I grabbed Keith's leg. The biggest ram was peering down at us from the rim, barely 40 yards away.

I rolled to my knees, knocked an arrow, and drew in one fluid motion. The gorgeous salt-and-pepper ram stood like a statue, unsure what the bizarre figures below him were. A split-instant later, my arrow smashed his chest like a hardball against concrete. He wheeled, faltered, then collapsed on a narrow ledge above a 200-foot cliff.

Never mind the hair-raising retrieval chore from that death-drop ledge. Never mind the stumbling nighttime back-pack to our tiny lakeshore camp. Even with one broomed horn, my 38½-inch x 33½-inch ram was a genuine grandpa with 11 annual growth rings, a gorgeous cape and a very high record-book score. As we roasted wild mutton on sticks the following day, I was thankful to be a sheep hunter.

A ROCKY MOUNTAIN BIGHORN

When I bowhunted Rocky Mountain bighorn sheep later that same year, I was rudely reminded how diverse sheep habitat and sheep hunting weather can be. Dall and Stone sheep conditions are relatively mild, because most hunting occurs in July, August and September. Most habitat is steep but eroded into traversable slopes.

My first exposure to Alberta's Canmore archery-only zone was a shock. Ice-covered mountains rose precipitously like the Swiss Alps from a low, narrow valley. Early-November temperatures were also scary—minus 25°F to minus 40 during midday. My guide Rod Collin and I grinned weakly at one another, loaded up 80-pound survival packs and climbed two miles up the steepest slope in sight.

Not all bighorn hunting is so severe. Seasons in some states and provinces begin in September, and terrain can be relatively easy to navigate. But the best bighorn hunting occurs during the November rut, when cagey rams leave thick timber and impossibly broken terrain to seek out more accessible bands of ewes.

Rocky Mountain bighorn rams love timber more than other types of sheep, especially where they are hunted hard. Even in lightly hunted lottery areas like Montana and Alberta, large rams spend most of their time in the trees.

A Rocky Mountain bighorn will stick to timber more than other species of sheep.

Understanding Sheep

Four species of sheep inhabit North America: the Rocky Mountain bighorn, desert bighorn, and Dall and Stone sheep. Sheep inhabit remote and primarily mountainous areas from Alaska and northwestern Canada, through the western provinces and states, down into Old Mexico. Like other sheep, our wild sheep are primarily grazers, preferring grass and forbs as forage most of the year, although in winter they will browse on shrubs if snow covers up the preferred foods.

All sheep possess superb eyesight, and have an excellent sense of smell. They don't rely heavily on their ears to warn them of danger, perhaps because rocks tumble and roll a lot in their steep, unstable habitat. Wild sheep may not be the most wary of North American big game, but they can be very difficult to hunt because they inhabit such remote, tough and broken terrain. Plus, it's often hard to find an old ram with truly oversized but unbroken horns, if you're after a trophy.

For my money, wild sheep are among the most beautiful of North American game animals, with well-muscled bodies that vary from lean to stocky, and gorgeous, curling horns that continue to grow throughout their life-time. Narrow growth rings on the horns mark each winter of a ram's life; if you're fortunate enough to kill a sheep, just count these rings to see how old he is! Any sheep of any variety is considered a monster if his horns measure more than 40 inches around the curl.

A Rocky Mountain bighorn will weigh anywhere from 160 to 300 pounds. His horns are massive, and handsome in contrast to his dark coat. A desert bighorn is lankier and lighter, weighing maybe 130 to 200 pounds and with a lighter coat; an adult ram's horns are big and thick too, and look almost over-sized compared to his smaller body.

Dall and Stone sheep are known as the thinhorn sheep. Dall sheep are pure white, and a good ram will weigh from 180 to 200 pounds; Dall sheep live in alpine grasslands above treeline, primarily in Alaska and the Yukon. Stone sheep vary in color, and you might see a gray, brown, white or even black animal. A good Stone sheep ram will be bigger than a Dall sheep ram—up to 250 pounds on the high end—and will be found in more steep, remote and isolated areas of the Yukon or British Columbia.

All sheep are magnificent, but so are the places sheep draw you to. This is a Rocky Mountain bighorn.

Dall sheep look spectacular in their white coats, but don't let that fool you: These sheep are hard to find and hard to hunt. You have to be in shape and ready to work.

A Rocky Mountain bighorn. Half the battle is drawing the tag to go after him. But the other half of the battle—actually getting him—is equally tough. You will work!

A Brutally Cold Hunt

Rod and I drew the short straw on our November outing. It was the coldest Canadian autumn on record. The limestone shoulders of sheep mountains were coated with ice, and the snow was crunchy as cornflakes. We set up our two-man expedition tent on a 6- by 8-foot slab of rock, dressed like two Michelin Men, and shivered through nine days of spot-and-stalk torture.

I have never been so cold. Bighorn hunting with rifle or bow requires hours of glassing until a mature ram pokes his nose from the timber. Shots are often longer than average for sheep, because opportunities are commonly across canyons. But prolonged subzero weather? Even my veteran guide had never seen hunting so grim.

To find bighorn rams you move and glass. You look long distances, and spend more time with spotting scope than with binoculars. These brownish critters are tough to see because of the trees.

I spotted my ram near dawn. He fed briefly, then bedded in a frozen meadow bounded by trees. I waited most of the day within 125 yards, shivering in nine upper-body garments and six pairs of thermal pants. When he finally stood up at sundown, I could hardly move. But I somehow lumbered to the cliff edge where he had disappeared, made the 25-yard, near-vertical shot … and watched in amazement as the ram slithered over a 450-foot cliff.

We recovered him the next day, using ropes and ice-climbing pitons. He was wrapped around a tree, his back broken in five places and his insides completely gone. Miraculously, the $10^{1}/_{2}$-year-old's horns and cape were beautifully intact.

The author packing out a bighorn.

Finding Rocky Mountain Bighorns

Some excellent bighorn sheep hunting can still be had in states like Montana, Oregon, Wyoming and Colorado. The trick is drawing a coveted lottery permit. British Columbia and Alberta still offer guided hunts for these incredible trophies on a first-come, first-served basis. The odds of bagging a ram are lower than the near 100-percent success enjoyed on Dall and Stone sheep. Trophy bighorns are fewer and farther between, inhabit nastier country, and present trickier shooting opportunities.

For my money, the Rocky Mountain bighorn is America's niftiest sheep. He's big and blocky, with the most massive horns. He oozes pure masculinity, especially during the peak of the rut when he slams horns with every other mature ram in his territory. He is our most difficult sheep to bag.

DESERT BIGHORNS

Desert bighorns are not easy to hunt. These slightly built, more drably colored brothers of Rocky Mountain sheep also carry immense, innertube-like headgear. Their hot, arid habitat can be a challenge—both to navigate and to find rams in as they feed, bed and rut. However, I must admit I especially enjoyed the shirtsleeve weather on an October desert bighorn bowhunt on northern Arizona's fabled Hualapai Indian Reservation. In this man's book, 60°F beats minus 30 by at least a mile!

It is commonly believed that desert bighorn sheep can only be hunted on coveted lottery permits in California, Arizona, Utah, Nevada and New Mexico. The fact is, several Indian reservations in Arizona sell desert sheep hunts to anyone who wishes to pay. Non-lottery hunts are also commonplace in Old Mexico. Ask a reputable booking agent for details.

A Rugged Hunt

My desert sheep bowhunt occurred in the most rugged terrain these animals inhabit. We were hiking and glassing atop the famed, 900-foot Red Wall of the Colorado Grand Canyon. Unlike other sheep, which normally look down for danger from on high, desert sheep in the Hualapai Grand

Desert bighorns live in some impossible-looking—but beautiful—places.

Canyon (and other such places) live below sheer bluffs in the bowels of cactus-choked canyons. They most often look up for mountain lions, men and other forms of danger.

What a guy won't do to shoot a desert bighorn!

My friend and internationally famous sheep guide Larry Heathington masterminded this hunt. Larry and guide Mario Bravo knew this area and knew desert sheep.

On day number one, I was surprised repeatedly at how difficult these animals were to see. Their dusty-colored hides blend with rocks and cactus to near perfection. Larry and Mario glassed downhill from rimrocks all day long, sweeping terrain like machines with their 10X Zeiss binoculars. Heat waves were so intense, our spotting scopes proved useless except at dawn and dusk.

The horns on a large desert ram completely overbalance his slender neck and body. We saw a dozen small rams and ewes during the first two days of the hunt. Most were in places accessible only by climbing rope. When the one and only big ram of that hunt materialized, I was blown away by his size. The horns curled bewitchingly backward and downward from the head like giant doughnuts, thrusting upward at the jawline in blunt, massively broomed stubs. Like all the other sheep we had seen, this ram's narrow bedding place was sandwiched between deadly high-dive cliffs.

Mario and I slithered down a 50-foot bluff on rappelling rope and inched along a foot-wide trail. Below us yawned the world's deepest and most dangerous canyon. I peeked around a 90-degree corner of rock, spied the ram behind a cactus, and noted that his huge left horn completely covered his eye. The rangefinder said 30 yards exactly, so I drew and shot immediately.

The 9¹/₂-year-old sheep leaped up, stumbled, and rolled. We retrieved him the next morning, after more rope climbing over 20- and 25-foot cliffs. Fortunately, the tumble did not ruin cape or horns.

A desert sheep hunter's best friends are a large canteen of water, a tube of sunscreen cream, and a wary eye for skin-impaling cactus. As in all forms of sheep hunting, comfortable hiking boots and good physical conditioning are a must.

Unlike other forms of sheep hunting, desert sheep rarely require overnight backpack camps or severe, long-distance hikes. Very few areas are as steep, dangerous and physically demanding as

The horns of desert rams look a little out of proportion—"big horns" like their name says—but quite a small body. (Because of their warm habitat, desert bighorns don't need to be as massive as their Rocky Mountain cousins to the north, who need to fight bitter cold and brutal snow.)

Three ways to get to sheep country: planes, horses and your own two feet. No matter how you get there, the journey is worth it.

northern Arizona's Grand Canyon. More typical desert sheep habitat is rough, semi-open and studded with cactus, but bluffs and slopes are navigable without ropes and a prayer.

THE KEY TO SUCCESS: PLANNING

Like all forms of North American big game hunting, finding trophy sheep of any variety is seldom easy. The best rams are hiding in places that people overlook. A wise sheep hunter does not blindly book a guide and expect wonderful results. He calls multiple outfitters and booking agents, asks for client reference lists, and spends plenty of time on the telephone. Even after the hunt is booked, he plans carefully with his guide. My most recent sheep hunt is a great example.

My dad and I had decided to hunt Dall sheep together. Dalls are the most abundant and most affordable of North American sheep, and after considerable research, I booked once again with my old pal Duane Nelson. His area in the Northwest Territories continues to produce nice rams, in large part because he limits harvest to 12 old, full-curl trophies per year.

Pop, at age 67, decided on a horseback hunt. He's a dyed-in-the-wool gun nut, and wouldn't think of touching a bow. His sheep rifle of choice was a Remington 7mm Magnum with a 4X scope and 160-grain bullets.

After talking to Duane, I decided to backpack from base camp to an area Duane had never hunted. It was a small mountain range so steep-sided there'd never been a horse or man on top. Duane suspected there were giant rams in the high basins where I was headed.

The results were exactly what we had hoped for. Pop and his guide rode their horses within half a mile of ten rams on a high slope, climbed for three hours, and dropped a full-curl beauty.

My hunt was enjoyable but more severe. Guide Lane Dyk and I climbed nearly 3,000 feet, often hand-over-hand. We weathered a late-July snowstorm in a sofa-sized tent, then sat in the fog for another full day. But on day number three, I went after my best-ever Dall, a 1½-curl beauty bedded high on a talus slope. Four hours later, in a drizzling rain, I bellied ahead, peeked over a rock and nearly dropped my teeth. The giant ram and seven others were up and feeding less than 50 yards away. Seconds later, I put an Easton XX78 arrow through both lungs. The ram was 11 years old, with horns just under 40 inches long.

As Lane and I gutted and quartered my ram, I could see the tiny white tents of base camp, some 12 miles and 8 hours of hiking below. I grinned and shook my head. What other hunting sport can be so physically demanding, yet give you such a thrill? 🐏

Sheep Hunting Equipment

The author, shown here with a desert bighorn, loves bowhunting for sheep and thinks they're an ideal archery animal if you're in-shape enough to handle the country. But physical limitations can be overcome; it will just be a different type of hunt.

More important than the specific rifle you take sheep hunting is how you use it. You may get one shot, after days of glassing and walking. Carry a rifle you can lug around comfortably for a long time, and be ready to make a tough shot count.

The same rifle you'd use for mule deer will work fine on wild sheep. Popular choices include the .270 Win. with 130-grain bullet, .30-06 Springfield with 150-grain bullet, 7mm Rem. Mag. with 160-grain bullet, and .300 Wthby Mag. with 180-grain bullet. Scopes in the 4X to 6X magnification ranges are ideal.

Contrary to popular belief, most rams are shot inside 150 yards with rifles. Terrain and your own physical limitations might require longer shooting. Since sheep prefer open or semi-open habitat, very long shots are commonly possible if you aren't inclined or able to stalk closer.

The average archery shot on sheep is 40 yards. These animals are not as hard-hunted or "wired" as some other species, making them ideal to bowhunt if you are in top physical shape.

Good-fitting mountain boots, top-notch 8X or 10X binoculars and a compact spotting scope are any sheep hunter's primary friends. For gun hunting, boots should have Vibram type lug soles for the best possible traction. For bowhunting, softer Neoprene or plantation crepe rubber allows quieter sneaking inside 50 yards.

Many hunts also require serious backpack equipment for day hikes or extended treks after trophies.

Weather can vary wildly on northern sheep hunts … even during summer months. Be prepared to dress in layers to accommodate heat, cold and wind.

Since most modern sheep hunts legally require a guide, ask your outfitter about specific hunting and shooting gear that works in his area. And don't be afraid to improvise. If you are in *great* physical shape, ask about places most guided hunters cannot or will not walk. If you are in poor health or don't feel physically fit, most top professionals can still recommend strategies that yield shots at rams. For example, horseback hunting is commonplace for Dall sheep in Alaska, the Yukon and the Northwest Territories of Canada, with nearly 100-percent success on full-curl rams. I once saw an 88-year-old man ride within 125 yards of a 38-inch Dall sheep. He climbed off the horse and knocked the sheep flat with one well-placed shot.

If you want to hunt sheep, age or physical condition are not necessarily obstacles.

Quality 8X or 10X binoculars are a "must" on every sheep hunter's equipment list. You'll spend a lot of time with them.

Chapter 11

Mountain Goats: Hunting Up Near Heaven

By Bob Robb

You'll have to be tough—and willing—to get to where he is. That's goat hunting.

Mike and I had climbed most of the morning and our legs were feeling it. Now we were bumping along the top of the mountain, peeking over from time to time in search of the bedded billies we'd spotted earlier. When we found one of them, he was basking in a sunbeam without a care in the world. I had dumped my backpack and begun the stalk when, for no apparent reason, the billy got out of his bed and moved slowly around the mountain.

Rats! I followed on hands and knees as fast as I could to the edge, then peeked over. There he was, downhill and 50 yards distant according to my laser rangefinder. I quickly nocked an arrow, settled the proper sight pin on his chest, and released. As the billy raced around the corner, I signaled to Mike to follow. He just smiled and pointed down below his perch, aimed the rifle at a spot I couldn't see, and fired.

Like my arrow, his bullet found its mark, and we had a pair of magnificent billies to admire first, then to cape, bone and pack back down to the base of a mountain surrounded by a sea of Alaska glacier ice. It was no easy task. Each billy weighed well over 250 pounds, yielding about 80 pounds of boned-out meat, plus cape and horns. We were two sore, tired boys that night!

That's mountain goat hunting for you. It's a tough game that involves lots of physical exertion and the ability to negotiate some of the continent's roughest areas. Often, the hardest part of bagging a good goat is being able to make the climb, being patient enough to let your billy get into a favorable position on the mountain, making the shot and then getting the harvested animal back down to civilization. And yet the animal itself, the country in which he lives and the many variables involved in pursuing him, make goat hunting special. If you love the mountains, goat hunting will surely grow on you.

Understanding Mountain Goats

Billies and nannies look very much alike. To identify a billy, look for heavier horn bases, horns that curve more, and belly fur that is stained or discolored (not as bright and white as what a nanny's might be).

Mountain goats live in the highest, most spectacular country available in Southern Alaska, coastal British Columbia, Yukon Territory, southwestern Alberta, and isolated parts of Washington, Oregon, Montana, Idaho, Utah, Nevada and Colorado. Goats are usually found at or above timberline. But in winter along coastal Alaska and B.C., snow can push them down almost to the beaches; in these regions they winter in the trees.

Early August hunting seasons find goats as high as they can climb, often above 10,000 feet. Their hair is also Marine Corps-short. As the season progresses, the animals come lower and their hair grows longer, reaching its most luxurious state in late October and early November. (Goats shed parts of their winter coats in summer.)

Summertime foods include grasses and forbs—explaining goats' liking of meadows—and in the winter, browse plants like willow and aspen become staples.

While both nannies and billys are usually legal (because they look so much alike), game managers strongly encourage taking only mature billies. Billies have heavier horn bases (though not always longer horns) and horns that curve back more than nannies'; also, a billy's belly fur may be stained or discolored.

In terms of trophy quality, any billy with horns exceeding 9 inches in length and bases of at least 5^1/$_2$ inches around is a good goat. An exceptional billy's horns will be closer to 10 inches in length and 6 inches at the base and will carry the weight all the way through. The difference between a good goat and an average one is often less than an inch of horn length and a half-inch of base diameter.

Billies are also larger and blockier of body, and at times they have a more yellowish coat than the whiter females. Billies tend to live higher on the mountain than nannies and kids. Mature goats stand 36 to 42 inches at the shoulder and are between 48 and 70 inches long. A nanny might weigh anywhere from 100 to 200 pounds, while a mature billy might go from 200 pounds to as much as 350.

All goats, young or old, male or female, are incredibly adept at negotiating steep, rocky terrain—even cliffs.

Goat horns aren't incredibly big: 9 inches with 5½-inch bases make a real trophy! Goat hooves almost act like suction cups and are perfectly designed for negotiating steep, rocky, rugged terrain.

Bob Robb, the author, displays a nice early-season goat. The animal's hair is shorter now than it would be later.

WHEN TO HUNT

In most areas, goat season is extremely long, allowing you great flexibility in your schedule. Early hunts conducted in August and early September generally favor the hunter with pleasant weather and long days, but you do have to deal with the occasional afternoon thunderstorm. Late September and October hunts feature turning colors, cooler temperatures and the chance of some snow. When goat seasons stretch on into late November and early December, as they do in parts of Alaska, you can be assured of lots of snow, wind and bone-chilling cold.

Most outfitted goat hunts occur in the midseason period, although many Alaskan outfitters offer early-season goat hunts, especially in southeastern Alaska where both goat populations and trophy quality are the state's best. Do-it-yourselfers, who either draw a limited-entry tag in one of the lower 48 states that offer goat hunting or are residents of Alaska and Canada, have more flexibility in their scheduling.

The later the hunting season gets—often on into November or December—the longer a goat's hair will get. Some hunters, like the author, believe this beautiful coat is a trophy equal to a billy's horns.

One consideration is the goat's hair. Early in the season, the hair is very short. By mid-October, it's long and lush, which makes for a more striking mount. In November, the hair is long, thick and most impressive. In my mind, a luxurious, thick coat is as much a part of a trophy billy as are his horns.

HOW TO HUNT

Regardless of whether or not you choose to hunt them early or late, remember that goats live in steep, often treacherous, country. In short, you can't be too physically fit to safely, successfully hunt them.

One time on a goat hunt in British Columbia, my guide and I spent four days riding horses around goat country, climbing steep, 45-degree slopes at least 2,000 vertical feet high two or three times each day before I finally shot a dandy billy. During that time, we looked over several different billies that looked great from the valley floor. But after climbing to within a quarter-mile of them and studying their horns closely through my 60X spotting scope, they just didn't quite cut the mustard. After it was all over, my guide told me that the base of the higher, tougher stuff.

Goats are as predictable in their habits as any animal I've ever hunted, unless bad weather sets in, in which case they'll head for the lee sides of mountains to avoid the wind. If they've been spooked by predators—including man—then goats will either head for the roughest, nastiest stuff around or exit completely and go to another mountain. If you spot a billy you like in a certain area one morning, chances are good he'll be very close to the same place the next morning, and the next, and the next. This makes it easier to plan and execute a stalk that may take some time.

The best way to stalk goats is from the top down. I always try and get above the goats, or at

You absolutely have to be physically fit to hunt mountain goats effectively. Walking and climbing are integral parts of the hunt.

most clients are completely whipped physically after one or two days of climbing. "If they would just get in decent shape, they would all have a good chance at an excellent billy," he told me. "Instead, after a day or two they're so tired and sore they'll shoot the first average billy we can get to, and be glad it's finally over."

Start Early, Glass Hard

It's wise to get into good goat country early in the day, then glass nearby peaks and ridges for the telltale white specks that turn into goats when you look at them through a powerful spotting-scope lens. Do this glassing before you climb to the top. In good weather, goats generally come down off the peaks to feed and water on adjacent ridges and gullies, then move back up to bed at

Start early, and glass upwards to the peaks and high ridges to try to locate goats before you make your climb for the day.

To complete a stalk, your best bet will be to climb, climb, climb and approach from above the goat. Consequently, most of your shots will be at some degree of downhill angle.

Crawl, creep, peek and sneak your way around goat country. You have to respect goats' eyes and noses, their primary defense systems, but don't ignore their ears either.

least on their level, before moving in. It seems like billies tend to look for danger from below, and are less likely to spot you if you can come in from above them. This is especially true if you are hunting with a bow and arrow.

The Nose & Eyes Will Bust You

Goats have a two-pronged defense system centered around their eyesight and sense of smell. If they smell you, they'll spook, although at times swirling mountain wind currents make it tough for them to pinpoint the location of the danger. If they see you—and stalking them over the open crags makes it difficult *not* to be seen—they may spook like scared rabbits. If the goats have been hunted little or not at all, they may simply saunter off, giving you time to make the shot.

Goats hear well too, and though they'll often ignore natural sounds like rolling rocks, human noises—like metal banging, loud voices and scratchy clothing scraping on sharp rock edges—can send them racing off.

As is the case with all big game hunting, however, the best way to approach a goat is without letting it see, hear or smell anything out of the ordinary. Use rock outcroppings, timber and natural gullies as your means of concealment when glassing for, then stalking, these animals; you'll up your odds for a good shot immeasurably.

goat permit in one of several lower 48 states. These permit hunts offer the enterprising sportsman who is willing to do some research a very good chance at good goat. The wild card then becomes—are you willing to work hard and get in real enough shape to be physically able to pack in and out of goat country?

Colorado, Montana, Wyoming, Idaho and Washington all offer great goat hunting and excellent trophy quality for those lucky enough to draw a tag.

I shot my first billy that way. Elk hunting one fall near Ennis, Montana, I'd seen some goats. Back at home I checked out the regulations and found there were a handful of permits issued for that area. I applied and luckily drew a tag that next year! My luck continued when, with the help of two friends and three horses, I managed to take a very nice billy with $9^1/2$-inch horns in one long but memorable day.

The author with a big Alaska billy. Alaska and British Columbia comprise the bulk of mountain goat country—and hunting opportunities—although you can hunt some mountain goats in the Lower 48.

WHERE TO HUNT

The best mountain goat country, with the highest goat densities and best overall trophy quality, is in the Far North, with Alaska and British Columbia leading the way. Nonresidents are required by law to hire an outfitter when hunting both areas. Mountain goat hunts are priced reasonably as these things go, with quality week-long hunts running in the neighborhood of between $3,500 and $4,500, excluding licenses, tags and transportation costs.

Those who wish to hunt goats on their own can do so by drawing a limited-entry mountain

Goat Trick

One trick I've used often while stalking goats is wearing a set of off-white coveralls, complete with white ski mask to cover my face. In my whites I can crawl around the rocks (never walk or stand up vertically in sight of goats while in your whites) and the goats have thought I was one of them long enough for me to get into position to shoot.

Always a Wilderness Experience

Mountain goats are the central figure in a true wilderness hunting experience that will never be forgotten. The country in which they live was created eons ago by glaciers, the same time period when scientists believe the goats themselves came to be. They have survived thousands of years with little change in either their physical makeup or character.

Spending time in the high peaks, dotted with pristine lakes and streams and rimmed with virgin timber, I always come away physically exhausted but spiritually refreshed. Mountain goats represent those ideals that drew me toward hunting as a youngster and that keep me involved today: unspoiled wilderness, which they must have to survive; a freedom of spirit unharnessed by outside influences; and a beauty I've seen matched in few places around the world.

These things draw me to goat country. When you hunt them for the first time, you'll know why I return year after year to climb and hike among spectacular peaks that help define my soul.

One thing about a mountain goat hunt is certain: You will experience some wild and unspoiled places. And that in itself will make any trip a success.

Equipment for Goat Hunting

Mountain goat country is tough, steep and rocky. Heed the author's advice on boots and clothing to ensure a good, comfortable trip.

Mountain goats are one of the toughest animals on the continent to cleanly kill. You want to carry enough gun or bow to anchor them.

I've taken two goats with a .280 Remington using handloads and the 160-grain Nosler Partition bullet, a combination that, together with rounds like the .30-06 and various 7mm magnums, I believe is the bare minimum. One of the .300 magnums is better still, and I have friends who wouldn't dream of hunting goats without their .338s. Use only premium quality bullets designed for maximum penetration, even when bone has been struck.

Goat rifles should be equipped with completely waterproof, fogproof scopes in the 2.5-8X, 3-9X or 2.5-10X class, that can take the bumping, banging, soaking and freezing they will invariably need to endure. A quality rainproof scope cover is essential.

Bowhunters are pursuing mountain goats more often these days, something I love to do. A couple years ago I shot a billy that officially scores 48⅞ Pope & Young points—which would place it in the top 20 ever taken with a bow—with a Mathews Z-Max single-cam bow set at 74 pounds, Beman ICS Hunter 400 carbon arrow, Barrie Archery Ti-125 broadhead and a rugged Sonoran Bowhunting Products pin-type bow sight.

Your standard deer hunting setup is plenty of bow. Use an extra-sturdy broadhead that can slice through a billy's thick hair and massive muscles.

Carrying a laser rangefinder makes lots of sense. Be prepared to shoot at a steep downhill angle.

Mountain hunting is an optics-driven game. You need high quality binoculars of at least 8X, and 10X is even better. A spotting scope with a top-end power of 45 to 60X is essential. Be sure to bring a sturdy tripod.

The right clothing is essential to both your comfort and safety in goat country. Dress in layers, starting with a synthetic wicking layer followed up with layers of fleece or wool. I prefer Gore-Tex and Windstopper fleece products, which are super lightweight and block 100 percent of the cold mountain winds. A packable Whitewater Outdoors Gore-Tex rain suit is always with me, as are a warm hat and gloves. A pair of rugged Gore-Tex boots with an aggressive sole (I like the airbob design best) are essential too.

Chapter 12

MUSK OX: ARCTIC ADVENTURE

BY JIM SHOCKEY

The Ice Age was a time of blistering cold and blinding snow. No summer, no spring for hundreds of years and then, finally, ice. Miles deep in some places, the polar ice cap crept across the land and destroyed everything in its path: wildlife, forests, hills, even mountains. Everything.

The mammoth died and so too did the cave bear, saber-toothed tiger and the woolly rhinoceros. They're extinct, petrified, all gone. Or almost all gone. One of the great shaggy creatures—the musk ox of pre-Ice Age times—survived and still survives today in the most remote place left on the North American continent: the Arctic.

Call me a romantic, but as a youth I remember standing on the icy prairies one pitch-black winter night thinking about hunting musk ox. The northern lights, though common enough on such a night, were pitching and heaving over my head, dancing more furiously than usual. Those lights seemed to beckon to me, bidding me northward. I made a decision that night: Sometime in the future I would make the journey to the Arctic, and when I did make that journey, I would hunt for a musk ox from the Ice Age.

Words like icy, bitter cold *and* isolated *only begin to describe what it's like to be in musk ox camp.*

Understanding Musk Oxen

Musk oxen survive some unbelievably brutal conditions, but the animals have a certain beauty all their own.

Ovibos moschatus, the musk ox, although resembling a bison, is actually more closely related to sheep and goats. Bulls reach a shoulder height of just over four feet and weigh up to 750 pounds. A cow will weigh 350 to 450 pounds. Their most visible features are their massive "bosses"—the horns that cap their foreheads in helmet-like fashion—and their shaggy coats. That coat consists of an undercoat of short, soft fleece, as fine as cashmere, and an outer layer of long guard hairs, some of which reach 25 inches in length. This incredible combination of hair allows a musk ox to withstand the brutal arctic cold and winds.

Musk oxen are grazers and will often move many miles in a day, in search of food. Winter finds the animals on windswept hills and slopes where vegetation is exposed; summer finds animals in grassy meadows and lakeshores.

Between 1700 A.D. and 1900 A.D., the musk ox population dropped to a barely viable low of 500 animals. Arctic explorers, on a single expedition, often killed several hundred musk oxen to feed their dog teams. Another cause for the declining

Summer musk ox band. The animals like lakeshores for the food there, and to escape the bugs a little bit.

population had to do with the commercial demand for musk ox hides that were used for sleigh rugs. The Hudson Bay Company alone shipped nearly 20,000 musk ox hides to Europe. In 1917, with the population in dire straits, the remaining musk oxen were deemed by the Canadian government to require complete protection.

This state of affairs lasted until 1967 when the musk ox herd was determined to be healthy enough once again to withstand a limited native harvest. Today musk oxen number nearly 100,000 in the Northwest Territories, sufficient to withstand not only a native harvest but a commercial and sport harvest as well.

A musk ox coat is long and shaggy, with an outer layer of guard hairs (some up to 25 inches long) and a soft and warm fleece undercoat. The original layering system!

THE LAST GREAT HUNTING ADVENTURE

ad·ven·ture n2 : an exciting or remarkable experience

That definition gets to the core of what musk ox hunting is about. It's not about treestands, cover scents and furtive animals. It's not about fancy lodges, permission and private land. It's about canvas tents and Inuit hunters, ice and snow, bitter cold and primitive creatures left over from the last Ice Age. It's about *adventure*.

First Hunt

Since that day over a quarter century ago, when I promised myself that I'd go musk ox hunting in the Arctic, I've been fortunate enough to go several times. And my highest hopes for adventure were always realized. The first trip—a late-fall excursion in the Arctic hinterlands—defined adventure. After dispatching a suitable musk ox bull with my Knight muzzleloader, a blizzard struck us hard. We struggled for five days to get back to the Inuit village before we were saved by a rescue party.

I wrote of that hunt, "Suddenly, wild and screaming like a banshee, the wind would hammer into our tent camp, forcing itself upon our small party of six adventurers. And so another time would pass, the three small canvas tents shuddering and heaving against their anchoring, every loose bit of tarp battering itself to shreds in the wind."

Adventure? Oh yeah.

An "Easier" Adventure

But the Arctic isn't always so inhospitably violent. My second trip—an early-spring venture—went smooth as ice. The stunningly beautiful Arctic world stretched white for a thousand miles in every direction. The sun warmed the barrenlands to a balmy minus 20°F, and the two other hunters and myself harvested three monster Boone and Crockett (B&C) record-book musk oxen. One was the second largest musk ox ever taken, while another placed in the number 21 spot. Mine, the

Author Jim Shockey with his record muzzleloader musk ox.

new world record for muzzleloader, would have placed in the number 10 spot in the all time B&C record book had I entered it!

HUNTING STRATEGIES & HOW-TO

Hunting a musk ox, besides the cost of the hunt itself, is an exercise in desire. If you're only half-willing to put in the effort to make it happen, it won't. Just researching the outfitters and selecting the one I considered to be the best took time and effort.

Eventually I narrowed my search down to one outfitter—Fred Webb of Webb Outfitting NWT Ltd., Box 313, Pritchard, British Columbia, V0E

2P0; (250) 577-3708, Fax: (250) 577-3740. Webb hunts out of Kugluktuk, Northwest Territories, in Canada; located on the shore of the Arctic Ocean, it's one of the easiest northern communities to access.

This alone saved me a fortune, but there were other reasons I chose this outfitter, safety being one of them. Webb stays in Kugluktuk, monitoring the radios in case of trouble. If an emergency arises, he's there to take care of it. Also, his Inuit guides are outfitted with Global Positioning System units (GPSs) and radios. Traveling out onto the icy tundra is undeniably spectacular, but is very, very unforgiving. Another reason I chose this area was because there is no commercial musk ox harvest.

On a typical musk ox hunt, expect to travel up to 100 miles the first day. The Inuit guide will drive the snow machine and the hunter will ride on the sleds full of camping equipment. For the duration of the hunt, home will be a canvas tent

Sneaking up on some musk oxen. They aren't difficult to get fairly close to. You just don't want to incite a charge!

You'll be hunting in an arctic wilderness, and you'll have to want to shoot a musk ox pretty bad. Conditions are tough!

heated by a Coleman burner. Food is a combination of "normal" food like eggs and sausages and "abnormal" food like boiled caribou and raw arctic char (there's plenty of "normal" food for those with tender tummies).

Most musk ox hunts take place in the spring (March and April) and are 5- or 6-day affairs. In a top-notch area, the hunter should see several musk ox bulls that qualify for the B&C record book! Old bulls tend to stick together in bachelor groups of two to a dozen animals, but occasionally will mix with the cows and calves. Typically, shots are 100 yards or less.

Musk oxen are not difficult to sneak up on, but care must be taken not to incite a charge. By many accounts, musk oxen attack the Arctic natives more often than polar bears do! Most times, when musk oxen feel threatened, the males will form the classic defensive circle: horns outwards, women and children protected in the center of the circle. This is good for judging the size and age of the larger animals in the herd, but bad for shot selection. Before the hunter can shoot, the musk oxen must disperse, thereby giving the hunter an unobstructed line-of-sight to the heart/

Modern snowmobiles are the most common mode of transportation in musk ox country (above). The land is so big and vast, you need to have a way to cover a lot of territory. Wind chill takes on real meaning when you're speeding across the snow-covered tundra. Here's what your chariot might look like (right).

lung region. A musk ox isn't particularly difficult to bring down, as long as the bullet or arrow is tucked in tight behind the shoulder.

MUSK OX DREAMS

My adventures in the north seem like dreams now. The musk ox, the ice and snow, the sleeping in a tent in the vast—absolutely vast—Arctic: Could it have been, all at once, so beautiful and harsh? Could it have been as utterly forbidding as I remember it and could the shaggy musk ox I hunted really have been so wild and primitive?

As I did nearly 25 years ago in the prairie night, I've made a decision: I'm going back again to find out.

Equipment for Musk Ox Hunting

When you hunt musk ox in the extreme, with icicles dangling from your cold nose, there is only one choice in clothing: Northern Outfitters expedition gear. All Northern Outfitters clothing and boots integrate their patented Vapor Attenuating & Expelling/ Thermal Retaining insulation for "extreme" cold weather (Vaetrex). It sounds fancy, and it is. The Northern Outfitters Scientific and Technical Advisory Board reads like the who's who in the relative fields of research: moisture condensation, nucleation and capillary theory. Contact: Northern Outfitters, 14072 South Pony Express Road, Draper, UT 84020-9570; (800) 944-9276.

Dressing properly is a survival thing, but for comfort, don't do a musk ox hunt without a good supply of disposable handwarmers. Hot Hands by Heatmax are an excellent choice. Contact: Heatmax Inc., PO Box 1191, Dalton, GA 30722; (800) 432-8629.

The musk ox hunter should also bring a bolt-action rifle, .270 Winchester or larger (prepped for cold weather by a gunsmith), a camera, a pair of binoculars, soft-shell rifle case and a pair of ski goggles. Everything else, including a sleeping bag, will be supplied by the outfitter. To avoid problems with condensation and lens fogging, firearms should be left in a case, outside. Don't worry about theft; there won't be any other humans within a long, bumpy, cold days' snowmobile ride.

If you go after a musk ox: Invest in proper clothing, including serious boots; have a gunsmith prep your rifle for extreme cold; bring plenty of handwarmers and a pair of ski goggles.

Chapter 13

WILD TURKEYS: BIG GAME BIRDS

BY GLENN SAPIR

*I*f you're thinking, "What's a bird doing in a book on big game hunting?" then you probably have never hunted the wild turkey. Let me illustrate.

An account of the first gobbler I ever shot could describe a hunt for white-tailed deer. Though the tactics would be considered somewhat unorthodox by today's accepted techniques, fall turkey hunting in New York's Catskill Mountains back then was a sport for which strategies were just being formulated and tested.

The mountain had been well scouted before the season began that Columbus Day. John Miller, one of my early turkey hunting mentors, was intimately familiar with the area and knew that a trio of gobblers frequently roosted in a stand of large pines. Some 50 yards uphill of the pines stood a wooden ladder treestand that Miller and his friends had traditionally used for deer hunting.

Guided to that stand, I began my ascent in the predawn darkness, and while doing so was startled to hear the flapping of wings from downhill; we had flushed turkeys roosting in the pines. Frustrated that I had scared the birds away before the hunt ever got a chance to unfold, I continued my climb to the platform in the tree. I pulled myself into position, tipped my cap to the departing Miller and loaded my shotgun.

Sensitive to every sound, I stood and waited. My tactics now were identical to a deer hunt that might take place from that same stand, but that day I was listening and watching for turkeys. The fog slowly dissipated as the sun rose to my right.

Off to my left, perhaps 200 yards away, I heard a yelp.

Inexperienced then as a caller and afraid a wrong note might alarm the turkey, I kept my box call handy, telling myself to use it only if necessary. For now, the tom was doing all the calling, coarsely yelping on occasion as he closed the ground between us. Ignorance prevented me from realizing that he was one of the gobblers I had unintentionally flushed from his roost. His approach seemed to be toward the breakup site, where he hoped to be reunited with his companions. But his route seemed to be uphill of the roost tree and would apparently take him into range of my 12 gauge.

The hairs on my neck stood up and my heart raced as my quarry approached the pines. Camouflaged in a woodland-patterned insulated jumpsuit—the only camo design of the time—I waited for the right opportunity to raise my gun into position. When the big, black bird entered the pines, I eased the shotgun up. I'm sure my nerves were frazzled, but nonetheless I steadied the gun.

When the turkey reappeared, I centered the bead on his head and fired. He dropped immediately and fluttered about. Not knowing that the turkey's gyrations marked his last breaths, I fired a second time.

The hunt could have been for a whitetail, and my excitement wouldn't have been any different. I kept telling myself, "You just killed a wild turkey, you just killed a wild turkey!" Before then, it was a

One of turkey hunting's biggest allures is that you can hunt both spring (left) and fall (right). On the left, author Glenn Sapir displays a spring Rio Grande gobbler from Texas. On the right, New York turkey hunter Bill Hollister with an autumn Eastern gobbler.

bird I knew of only through magazine pages.

I have hunted turkeys with dedication ever since, expanding my success to the more popular spring season. My knowledge of the bird and turkey hunting tactics has increased immeasurably over the years. So has my respect for our big game bird, the wild turkey.

In fact, a turkey hunting passion has grown in me. I even achieved the Grand Slam by harvesting four subspecies of wild turkeys in one spring. Yet, for the turkeys I've shot and all I've learned in many years of countless hunts for this feathery creature that flies, I still think of the wild turkey as a big game animal.

FINDING PLACES TO HUNT

As with virtually any big game hunting, the initial turkey hunting challenge is finding a place to pursue your quarry. Public land is a viable option but often isn't available. The work involved in identifying land, gaining access and scouting the property is your responsibility, and is an integral part of the hunt.

With turkey hunts occurring in every state but Alaska, you may not have to look far beyond your own state or even county to do your turkey hunting. During the course of the year, you may see turkeys in fields or crossing roads. Don't hesitate to ask anyone you know, especially mail deliverers and parcel couriers, where they may have seen birds. Keep your ears alert for comments at parties or in line at the supermarket.

I recall picking up some clothes at the dry cleaner's one day. The proprietor knew I was bonkers over turkeys and asked me when the season was to open. The other customer in the store blurted out that he always saw turkeys on his property.

We exchanged some other small talk and I said

good-bye. Later that day I called the dry cleaner and asked for the name of that customer. In minutes I was calling the gentleman, reintroducing myself and making an appointment to come by to scout the property.

"Of course you can hunt," he said over the phone that day. Though it wasn't the hot spot he painted it to be, I did have a lengthy conversation with a reluctant tom one morning. And two years later, that property rewarded me with a beautiful adult gobbler on the next-to-last day of the spring season.

The moral of the story: Keep your ears open, and alert all of your acquaintances to the fact that you are looking for places to hunt turkeys.

Once you have identified a potential place to hunt, secure permission. That may mean simply a phone call to start, but most landowners prefer to meet the person who wishes to hunt on their land. When you meet the landowner, make a good impression. No, you don't have to wear a jacket and tie, but camouflage clothing is not recommended. Let him or her know that you are a longtime hunter and that you value safety and respect for property over all else. If they seem to be reserving access, offer to do some kind of work in exchange for permission. Anyone—especially an active farmer—with any amount of land has plenty of chores that need doing. Always follow up at the end of the season with a thank you card, and remember the landowner with a holiday card as well.

SCOUTING

Once you have options on hunting lands, you want to narrow down choices to areas that are most worthy of your efforts. Let the landowner (or public land staff) point you in the right direction. Then your ears and eyes will take over the scouting.

What every hunter is looking for: Some good land that turkeys call home. Finding places to hunt is really the true first step of any successful turkey hunt.

Understanding the Wild Turkey

Gobblers "gobble" to announce their presence and attract hens (the hens are supposed to go to the gobbler in the scheme of things). Then the male struts, drums and spits, fans his tail and displays for hens, all to show off and convince a potential mate that he's the one for her. These turkeys are Rio Grandes.

The United States wild turkey population dropped to an all-time low of 30,000 birds in the 1930s, when the bird had disappeared from 18 of the 39 states and the only Canadian province it had once inhabited. Conservation practices, spearheaded by wildlife departments and the National Wild Turkey Federation, along with much land reverting back to forest and live trap-and-transfer successes, aided in the bird's remarkable comeback. Today wild turkeys are hunted in all of the states except for Alaska, and in four Canadian provinces. They number more than 4.5 million.

You'll find the Eastern subspecies across much of the U.S.

Closely related Osceola turkeys inhabit Florida. Rio Grandes inhabit the open country of eastern Colorado down through Texas. And the handsome Merriam's is a bird of the West.

A gobbler's beard. No one knows its biological use for sure, but for hunters it's one of the trophies of the hunt.

Big Game Wisdom

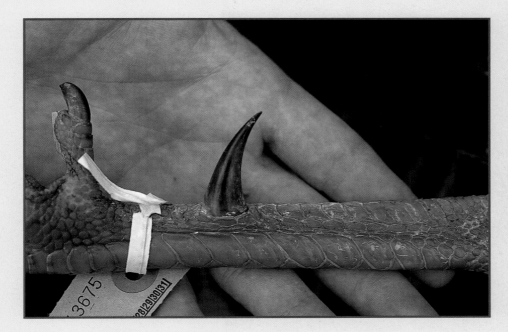

A gobbler's spurs are made for fighting. Competition among gobblers ensures that the strongest and most virile toms breed with the hens.

The wild turkey is a challenging game bird. Its size is impressive. An eastern gobbler in the corn-belt may reach 30 pounds. Hens more typically weigh 10 to 12 pounds.

Though a small percentage of hens, perhaps 5 percent, exhibit a beard, which is a bristly protrusion from the chest, it is every gobbler's badge. Hunters put stock in three measurements of a gobbler: its weight, the length of its spurs, and the length of its beard.

Though the function of the beard is unknown, the spurs contribute to the gobbler's self-defense system. Its long, strong legs, unlike those of its domestic counterpart, are built for running and quickness, which aid its escape from predators. Its wings are not just ornaments, as they've become on the fat, nonflying domestic birds. Turkeys will not only fly to and from their nighttime roosts, but they will escape danger by taking wing. An uncanny sense of hearing allows turkeys to home in on seductive calling, by both hens and hunters, and helps them to detect danger as well.

Even more remarkable, perhaps, is the bird's sense of sight. A turkey can see well for long distances. Also valuable in its self-preservation is the bird's ability to detect movement. Hunters attempting to make yelps with handheld calls, or to slip shotguns into position, have sent many gobblers packing.

For all its life, a turkey is sought by predators. Snakes, raccoons, foxes, skunks and other wildlife covet turkey eggs. The young are no less desirable, sought after by raptors as well as land predators. Coyotes, bobcats and lions will tackle adults. Nevertheless, turkeys survive throughout the year, and many grow to maturity. It is for those males in the spring of the year that man becomes a predator.

Mature toms feed little in the spring, living off a sponge of breast fat. They seek to breed with as many hens as they can, using all their male attributes to win them over. A heart-jolting gobble tells nearby hens that the tom is ready to pass along his genes. His posture of spreading his tail feathers into a giant fan, and puffing out his chest and lowering his wings by his side, all present an image of a muscle man at the beach strutting for a bikini-clad woman.

The resonance of the gobble, the image of the tom in strut, and the challenge of bringing him into gun range all make hunting the wild turkey in spring a memorable challenge.

Use your ears to scout. What do you listen for? Gobbles! Short of seeing the bird, it's the only surefire way to know a gobbler is nearby. Merriam's tom gobbling (left).

You'll also use your eyes to scout. These turkeys (below) are in their roosting tree. Be out at dusk to try to locate birds flying up to roost.

Scouting: Listen

First, you'll use your ears to scout. Listen for the distinct gobble of the tom and the yelps of both sexes. Early morning in the weeks leading up to the spring hunting season, when the birds' mating instincts are awakening, is the best time to listen for the yelping of the hens and, more importantly, the gobbling of the toms. These vocalizations will assure you of the presence of wild turkeys, and also help you pinpoint roosting areas, which will become the focal points of your hunts. Dusk, when birds go on roost, is another good opportunity to listen for wild turkeys.

It may not be necessary to call to locate birds, though various sounds (produced naturally or by you) may draw a shock gobble. A shock gobble can best be explained as a gobble made in reaction to a loud sound. It occurs most often when toms are in the mating mode, and they may gobble from trees or on the ground to owl hoots, crow caws, goose honking, peacock shrieks, coyote howls, car horns, gunshots, other gobbles and almost any other loud sound. In the case of the "dry cleaner gobbler," the tom revealed his presence first by answering a hen yelp I had emitted, then seconds later by sounding off to the 10:00 siren from the firehouse in a hollow a few hundred yards away.

Here are three types of turkey sign you can look for, to see if birds are in the area. A gobbler's droppings (top left) will be J-shaped. Tracks (top right) show where turkeys have been traveling. You'll also want to look for scratchings and turned-over leaves on the forest floor. An area where turkeys have dusted (above) is also great sign.

Scouting: Look

Sight is another key sense for scouting. Of course, you may get lucky and see birds. Gobblers will often select open areas, such as farm fields and power line openings, to strut in view of prospective mates. If you have an idea of where birds are roosting, you may watch at dusk just before and as they fly up to their nighttime perches. In the spring, toms feed little, concentrat-

ing their waking hours and energy on mating. In the fall, however, toms will typically band together and can be spotted feeding, especially in cultivated fields where manure, containing undigested grain, has been spread.

Short of seeing actual birds, you might spot telltale signs of their presence. Scratchings—areas where leaves have been turned over or soil raked—indicate that turkeys have been searching for food. Scratching done close to the base of trees has most likely been done by toms. Dusting areas, which resemble small deer scrapes, show where birds wallow and beat their wings in a dust bath to rid themselves of annoying bird lice and other parasites. Sometimes the birds leave behind feathers and tracks in the dust. Both tracks and feathers reveal a turkey's presence and can also hint at the sex of the bird.

A tom's tracks are larger than a hen's, and so is the distance between tracks; in other words, a gobbler takes longer strides. A gobbler's track, from front to back at its longest point, will be greater than $4^1/2$ inches; a hen's will be less. A tom's body feathers have shiny black tips; a hen's have buff-colored tips.

Another sign that turkeys have been nearby is scat. The female's is round; the tom's is a distinctive "J" shape. When you find several droppings in one place, you may have discovered a roosting tree.

Another way to home in on likely turkey-holding areas is to identify favored food sources. Wild turkeys are extremely opportunistic eaters. They have been known to eat more than 400 different foods—both animal and vegetable matter. Grasshoppers are a favorite, for instance, and fields that support large populations of those insects likely could serve as feeding and displaying areas. Hardwoods produce the mastcrop, both hard and soft, that wild turkeys may thrive on, and if you find stands of oak, beech, cherry, maple and other food-producing trees, investigate the area for scratching and other signs of turkey activity. It may pay off to contact the state wildlife agency, and see if a publication or a biologist there can help you identify favored foods in the region you'll be hunting.

DRESSING THE PART

You don't have to look like a model in a turkey-hunting catalogue, but you should camouflage yourself from head to toe.

I remember one opening day of deer season, when a group of about 25 roosting turkeys flew down at dawn and wandered toward me and the tree against which I stood. I had on a hunter-orange cap, but they never noticed it. They literally surrounded me and ignored me as they fed along the ridge.

Yet these birds were not warily coming into an unseen hen's calls, as would be the situation in the spring when a tom would be looking hard for the yelping hen, uncomfortable perhaps in the scenario that conflicts with the typical mating ritual. (Normally, it is the hen that approaches the tom's calling and displaying.) So if you want to up your odds, you'll wear good camouflage.

Your shirt, jacket, pants and a cap should all be of camo. Though the need for a particular camo pattern may be made more significant through marketing than reality, a camouflage that best blends in with the habitat of your hunting area is preferable. In the South, that may favor more green than brown. In northern locales, especially early in the spring season, brown may work best. Mixing colors can help you break up your outline in the woods, which is one of camouflage's prime functions. Wearing predominantly brown camo pants and green camo upperwear can help you match the brown of the ground and the green of emerging vegetation.

The Turkey Hunting Vest

Every turkey hunter needs a vest to carry all the necessary "stuff."

Invest in a turkey hunting vest. It is your portable filing cabinet. Ideally, it will have either custom pockets for box and slate-type calls, or ample nonspecific pockets to store them. It must have a game bag that is easily cleaned, and it should have some kind of hunter-orange panel that you can fold out if you are walking through the woods and wish to reduce the chances of being mistaken for a turkey by another hunter. Because you also may be toting additional shotgun shells, drinks, snacks, decoys, pocket cameras, raingear, insect repellent, gloves, toilet paper, first-aid supplies and other accessories, you need plenty of storage space.

Be prepared for the elements and local conditions. This means adding raingear (that is both camouflage and quiet); you can't use it if you don't have it with you. Some hunters improvise by cutting holes out of a large green garbage bag, but the crinkly noise may be prohibitive. One important accessory is a waterproof cushion. Attach it to the vest or clip it to a belt loop. It will provide comfort that can translate into longer, quieter sitting when you set up on a gobbler.

Wear camouflage, head to toe, on any and every exposed area—right down to your T-shirt, socks, face and hands.

Clothing Details

Turkey hunting is a detail game, and there are other considerations for clothing.

Starting from the bottom, wear camo-patterned or brown boots, and make sure their heels and soles are dark. Sitting next to a tree, emitting turkey calls to lure in a gobbler, makes you the focus of concentration. A light sole could suggest a gobbler's head to a hunter; it could suggest a poorly dressed hunter to a gobbler.

Wear dark socks. When you sit against a tree, your pants may ride up and reveal the light socks (turkeys will see them) or the dangerous red or blue colors of athletic-sock striping, colors also found on the gobbler's head. For the same reason, long underwear should be camo or green. Belts should be brown, black, green or camo, and the buckle should be a nonshiny color and finish. If your shirt or jacket is open on top, wear a round neck, camo undershirt.

Between your cap and your collar should be a head net that you can slip up into place easily. Nets that cover your neck add camouflage. Those with a wire frame around the eye area allow you to bend the frame to customize the openings for optimum comfort and concealment.

Head nets may still leave some skin visible around the nose and eyes, though. Consider using camo paint in those areas to enhance your concealment.

THE HUNT: SPRING

With preseason arrangements made and gear in order, you are ready. Though no two hunts will unfold identically, you should have a basic idea of a typical hunt scenario to master the finer points of turkey hunting.

Put Them to Bed, Get Out Early

If the opportunity presents itself, go to (but not in) likely roosting areas at dusk. Listen and watch for turkeys flying up into the trees for the night. The next morning before light, if you have "put a gobbler to bed," return to within 100 to 200 yards of the location, trying to stay uphill or at least on the same level as the ground where the bird is perched. Approach carefully and quietly so you don't spook or alert the birds!

If you didn't roost a bird the night before, go to areas that showed promise when you scouted. Before first light, while the turkeys are still in the trees, hoot like an owl with your voice or an owl call, imitating a barred owl. A tom on roost will often answer with a shock gobble. When you get a response, quickly and quietly get yourself into position within 100 to 200 yards of the believed roosting area; try to remain uphill of, or on the same level as, the tom.

Then make soft tree yelps with any of a variety of calls (see pages 196–198). Your goal is to imitate a hen that is nearby. Make these calls quietly and infrequently, especially once you've gotten a gobble in response.

Now, await fly down. I like to encourage fly down by using an actual turkey wing, a commercially available substitute or simply slapping my thigh repeatedly with my hunting cap to imitate the sound of a hen flying down. When the gobbler flies down, you may hear his wing beats and may even see him hitting the ground. At other times, the bird may hit the ground without you knowing it, and either vocally signal his approach with gobbles or silently sneak in toward the hen you have portrayed. Be ready at all times; he won't necessarily make a racket coming in!

Your job is to keep that bird coming toward you until he presents a clear shot at the head/neck area, within 40 yards. Though turkeys have been killed at greater distances, you will want to seek even closer shots, which help ensure a clean kill and a successful hunt.

This hunter, positioned uphill from a roosted gobbler, is yelping on a box call. If you get a response, be cagey: Calling quietly and infrequently is often the best plan.

Setting Up

For a hunt to unfold smoothly, you must be conscious of every action you take leading up to the shot. For instance, as you set up, be aware of physical barriers that could be obstacles between you and the bird. Fences, especially high- or woven-wire types, may discourage an approach into range; so might a wide expanse of water. Though turkeys will cross small creeks, they may not choose to fly across wider water courses.

When selecting a place to set up, look for a wide tree, broader than yourself if possible, to help camouflage and break up your outline. Sit against the tree, knees up, to provide a rest for a possible shot. If the stand of trees leads to a clearing that lies between you and the gobbler, don't sit against the tree closest to the clearing. It will not camouflage you as well. A good tree allows you a shot within range as soon as the tom becomes visible. That might mean setting

Decoys can improve your odds of getting a gobbler to come in to your setup. A hen (shown) is essential, because a gobbler wants to see the object of his affection.

A jake decoy could be just the thing to make your setup perfect and bring that gobbler all the way in. A big old gobbler will resent the young turkey and will come in aiming to thrash the jake and drive him off.

up farther back from the field, in a stand of trees that will present a shot when the tom comes into the grove looking for the hen.

On the other hand, toms are used to being able to see their would-be mates. Portable decoys can help. Many manufactured decoys are foldable and portable, and can easily be set up and secured to the ground on portable stakes. If you plan to use decoys, a hen model is essential. It represents the bird the hunter has pretended to be. Place it within 20 yards of your tree. Adding a jake decoy—that is, a deke painted like a 1-year-old male—might bring out the aggressive dominance of a gobbler and lure him right in. He may get mad enough to come in to thrash that interloper. Be sure to check hunting regulations for your state to verify that decoys are legal.

Moving on Birds

Turkey hunting often becomes a waiting game, a battle of patience as a gobbler "hangs up" out of range, waiting to see "the hen" from a vantage point at which he feels safe. Or he might just give up and move off, gathering the hens he has already amassed. Or, he might leave to seek other prospective, easier mates. Then you must make a decision. Do you stay still, hoping to lure in the hung-up bird? Or do you move, following the bird or possibly cutting off his route?

Be warned! Many times a hunter will get up, giving up on a bird, only to discover that the tom had silently circled behind and was silently coming to the calling from another direction. That's the chance you must weigh. So if you do decide to

Before you move on a bird because you don't think he will come in, take some time to double-check the situation. That gobbler may have just gone silent or may be sneaking in from another direction.

setup might be best. This way the hunters can readily communicate to each other with whispers and concealed elbows. If only one of you is to shoot, the other might serve as the caller, as well as provide a pair of experienced eyes.

Agree on a landmark directly in front, usually a tree, as 12:00. Then, by equating the time on the clock with the position of an approaching turkey, you can more clearly and with fewer words communicate the bird's location. If both hunters are shooters too, then the 12:00 landmark could serve as the divider between each person's shooting territory. Or, if both hunters are planning on shooting, you might also sit back-to-back on opposite sides of the tree. This visually covers more ground and is a safe technique as well.

If only one hunter will be shooting, the companion may choose to call from perhaps 20 to 40 yards behind him. Why? Because sometimes gobblers, when they get to within the distance at which they believe they should be seeing the hen, won't budge. This is called "hanging up." If the caller sits well behind the shooter, that point of hangup, otherwise called a strutting line, may fall within shooting range.

move on a bird you suspect may still be nearby, be quiet, keep a low profile and cut a wide trail from the gobbler's route. You cannot overestimate the sight and hearing of a tom that has been brought to full alert.

When trying to cut off a bird or simply get closer, utilize natural and artificial features of the landscape, be it a stream bed, a gully or draw, a hill … any landscape feature that will hide your movement. In my "home" turkey woods of the Northeast, 100-year-old stone walls, built by farmers, serve me well for this purpose.

Hunting in Tandem

The safest way for two hunting companions to pursue turkeys is to hunt together. One may call and the other shoot, or they both may take on the double duty.

If a novice is afield with a more experienced hunter, a side-by-side

There are many cases when setting up with a partner makes turkey hunting sense.

The Weather Factor

Don't let rain, snow or any other inclement weather stop you from turkey hunting. There are only so many days to hunt ... and the turkeys are still out there, no matter the weather!

Turkeys live outside 365 days a year. Inhospitable weather is more likely to keep you out of the turkey woods than it is to spoil your chances for success. But certain weather conditions might dictate how you hunt gobblers.

For example, rain seems to bring birds into fields. If you want to stay dry and play the odds on a rainy day, try setting up a blind at the edge of a field that birds have been known to frequent.

A snowstorm, which can occur during turkey season in many states, might drive birds to thick cover. If you don't find action in typical spots, seek thick stands of conifers, laurel and other places where turkeys might escape the brunt of the storm.

Wind is the worst weather condition for turkey hunting. For one reason, calls might not travel far in the noisy, interfering gusts.

Similarly, a turkey's response to your call, or a gobble set off by another stimulus, may be difficult for the hunter to hear. Finally, turkeys (like other big game animals) depend on their senses, including hearing, to survive. When an animal's hearing is impaired, it becomes more wary and less active than usual. So it is with a turkey. As with rainy conditions, turkeys may gather in low, protected areas where the wind is not as much of an adverse factor. If favored hunting areas don't pan out, seek areas protected from the strong winds.

Heat is an uncomfortable situation for both turkey and hunter. Just as you would seek shade on a torrid day, so will the turkey. Remember this and go to shaded hillsides and thick timber instead of sun-exposed fields, when the temperature gets too hot to handle.

Turkey seasons are too short for you, the hunter, to be picky. Though weather conditions may not be perfect, simply size up the situation and make the most of it. Differences between the run-of-the-mill turkey chasers and the expert gobbler hunter are certainly knowledge and experience, but another key difference is effort. The person who does his homework and "goes to school" on past hunts, books, magazines, videos, seminars and friends, and applies that data bank every opportunity possible, is the one who will truly possess turkey hunting wisdom.

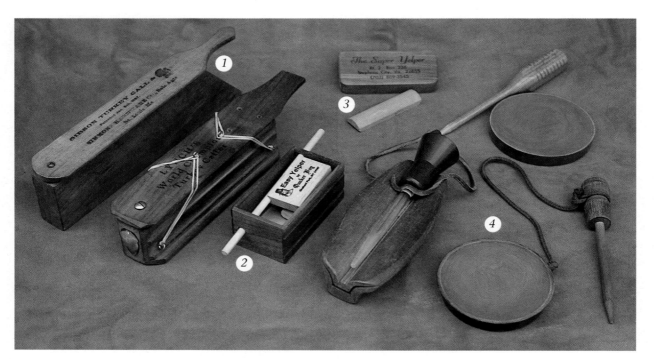

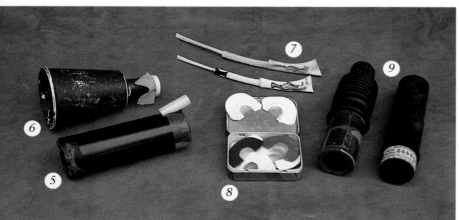

Turkey calls come in two forms—friction calls (above) that you operate by hand, and mouth calls (left). Friction calls (above) include (1) box calls, (2) push-button yelper, (3) super yelper and (4) peg-and-slate calls. Mouth calls (left) include (5) tube call, (6) owl hooter, (7) wingbone calls and (8) diaphragm calls. Gobbler shakers (9) that imitate a tom's gobble are another hand call.

TURKEY SOUNDS & CALLS

Turkeys make a variety of sounds, and you, as the hunter, need to know the basics of each one and what it means. You'll also want to learn to create these sounds yourself, and will need calls to help you do it.

Locator calls could mimic a coyote, a goose, a peacock, a crow, an owl or a variety of other creatures. The barred owl hoot (in the traditional "Who cooks for you, who cooks for you all" cadence) is the most popular call for drawing a shock gobble, especially while the birds are still on roost. Crow caws are a popular locator in daylight conditions. Locator calls are valuable because they may tip you off to a gobbler's location, yet they

will not draw the gobbler toward you as a hen yelp, cluck or purr might. This gives you a chance to determine the general location of the gobbler and work toward him, before selecting a good setup spot.

A gobble, which can be made with a box call, a gobbler shaker or natural voice, can also serve as a valuable locator call. In addition, when all else fails to bring a gobbler into range, you can incorporate a gobble into your performance after emitting some hen calls. This gobble represents competition for the reluctant gobbler, and might be enough to draw him into range.

Both gobblers and hens yelp and cluck. The gobbler's sounds are coarser than the hen's. Clucks are short "one-syllable" calls that show contentment and location, letting the calling bird know that it is here. Yelps are typically vocalized in a series, and they more aggressively announce to the world that a bird, usually a hen, is here. The more emphatic the yelping, the more enamored the hen is portrayed to be.

Cutting is an irregular series of yelps that seem to cut into one another. This is even more aggressive than normal yelping, and suggests that a hen is romantically excited and eager to be bred.

Purrs are soft, drawn out calls that show contentment and desire. They are often the final punctuation on a long hunt. Their plaintive sounds may be irresistible to a lovelorn gobbler. Challenge purrs play on the dominance of a gobbler.

Cackles are a quick series of calls made by birds when they fly up to roost and down from their roost. Identifying cackles will help you locate birds at prime time as the hunting day begins or at night, setting the stage for an eventful next-morning outing.

Many different callers exist, including those made from the wing bones of the turkey itself. The most popular for novices is the box call and its variation, the one-handed yelper; these may be the easiest of all calls to master. But their ease should not belie their effectiveness. Many hunters use only a box call, with which they can emit virtually any sound a turkey makes, including a gobble.

Another basic kind of friction call is the peg-and-slate. It is a round call that fits in the palm of the hand. With the other hand, a peg (or striker) is rubbed at a 45-degree angle to the surface. With this caller you can mimic clucks, yelps and purrs in an extremely realistic fashion. Some callers substitute glass or aluminum for different pitched sounds.

The diaphragm call slips against the roof of your mouth. It produces authentic-sounding calls

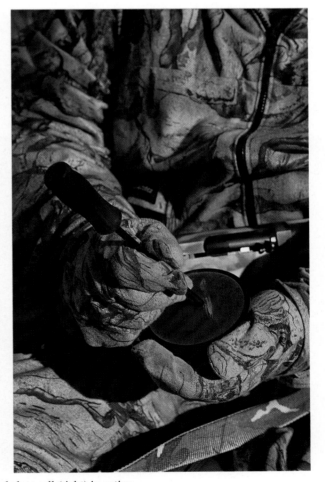

A box call (left) and a peg-and-slate call (right) in action.

A hunter calling with a diaphragm call. Diaphragms are hardest to master, but they can produce incredibly turkey-like sounds.

Fall turkey hunting often depends on scattering the birds far and wide, then setting up to call them back in. A decoy can help you convince an incoming bird to come all the way in to join the gathering group.

and also leaves your hands free. This is vital when the gobbler is nearing gun range because any hand movement (either from making a call or raising your gun) might be spotted by a tom looking hard for his vocalizing "mate." And a cluck on a mouth call might be all that is needed to get a turkey to raise his head after you have readied your gun for the shot.

You will find other calls too, many of which are effective. But if you can master the box, slate and diaphragm, along with a few key locator calls, you will have the key calling skills needed to bring in a gobbler.

Videotapes, audiotapes, books, magazines, calling contests—and time in the turkey woods—will all contribute to the learning process and help you improve your calling skills. And remember: The time to practice calling is not when you have a gobbler somewhere out in front of you. Practice— a lot—year-round.

FALL HUNTING

By autumn, turkeys generally have banded into social groups for colder weather—gobblers with gobblers, jakes with jakes and hens with other hens and their young of the year. Figure out their roosting and feeding patterns to find these birds. Though toms may gobble at any time of the year, the spring tactic of yelping (like a hen) to locate a mature male rarely will reap rewards.

Where autumn hunting is legal, most states allow the harvesting of any turkey; in spring, the usual legal qualifier is a bird with a visible beard. In the spring you will hunt with ears first, eyes second and legs third. In the fall, the order will reverse. Though turkeys will continue to communicate with each

Finding the food is key to finding autumn turkeys. Soft mast (like these highbush cranberries, above) and hard mast (such as these acorns, right) are key. Soft mast will be important earlier in the fall (as will grasshoppers and other insects), while the hard mast will come into play later. Harvested crop fields also attract birds.

other through vocalizations, it is more likely that a lot of walking will eventually let you spot a bird (or more likely a group of turkeys) before you hear one. Though adult gobblers are not very vocal, coarse clucks and yelps can bring them in. Patience is paramount. Once you locate the birds you may try to shoot one as it comes into range.

But many fall turkey hunters prefer to scatter a flock, and then rely on the gregarious birds' desire to regroup to call one into shooting range. Shooting over the birds will often help get a good scatter; a good scatter is one in which birds go in many different directions, so they have to work to regroup.

Immature birds, unable to project full-blown yelps, will make a kee-kee. This whistling sound, followed by a weak yelp, signals the bird's approach to the original breakup site. Mimic this kee-kee, as well as the mature hen's yelps, to bring the birds back together at the point of scatter. You might want to sit uphill from that point, as turkeys like to approach that spot from above so they can look for the danger that flushed them.

In some states in the fall, hunters can legally use dogs; their purpose is to find the turkeys and scatter them. Canines, some bred for this purpose, can be extremely effective at setting up the calling phase of the hunt.

Safety First

The most important element of any hunt is safety. If an accident occurs, nothing else matters. So remember these tips:

- Positively identify your target. Be double sure that it is a gobbler you are shooting at, and that no other hunter is in the line of fire.
- When you are set up and another hunter walks onto the scene, signal him by yelling. Do not wave, whistle or, worst of all, use a turkey call.
- Don't stalk a bird. Call him to you. By stalking, you may be putting yourself into the line of fire of another hunter who is working the gobbler you are sneaking up on. Furthermore, by stalking and calling, you may suggest that you are a turkey to a nearby hunter.
- Sit against a tree or other object wider than you. Not only does it camouflage you well, but it also protects your back from a hunter who may be working the same bird as you.
- Wear camouflage clothing, and do not wear or carry *anything*—even socks—that has red, white or blue. Wear dark socks instead of white ones, and wear a camouflage T-shirt.

A key to finding birds in the fall is knowing where they are feeding. Scouting for signs of scratching, as well as for potential food supplies, can be important to a successful hunt. Early autumn is when turkeys are feasting on grasshoppers in fields. Next on their menu as the calendar turns is soft mast. Later they will turn to hard mast. Harvested crop fields will also attract birds, as will manure spread on fields (turkeys come to pick out the undigested grain).

Find the food and you'll likely find fall turkeys.

TRULY A BIG GAME BIRD

Turkey hunting is big game hunting. A strutting, gobbling full-grown gobbler is an impressive sight indeed. He may weigh only a fraction of what some of our other, more traditional big game animals weigh, but I guarantee he will make your heart race, your palms sweat and your knees weak when he gobbles back at you and then comes strutting and spitting to your calls.

And you will work hard to get a good turkey—and any legal turkey is a good one. You will work to locate a hunting spot, practice calling until your family wants to kick you out of the house, scout intensely for birds, get up many hours before dawn for many mornings to hunt, and even go home empty-handed most of the time. But, every once in a great while, everything will come together just so and you'll come home with a turkey. All the work will all be worth it and you'll start counting the days until you can go turkey hunting again.

If that's not big game hunting, I don't know what is!

Hunting turkeys is as exciting and rewarding as any hunting in North America. These magnificent birds truly deserve status as "big game."

Equipment: Turkey Guns

Knowing how your shotgun shoots with different loads and identifying the load that performs best is a required step before any turkey hunt.

Your choice of shotgun is personal. Though some hunters want all the firepower they can get—shooting a 10 gauge with magnum loads—others challenge their skills by hunting with a 20 gauge or even a .410. But for my money, the 12 gauge, chambered for 3-inch loads, is an effective choice. Choked full or extra-full, the 12 gauge can do all you would ask of a turkey gun. In many states, your shot size is limited to a range, perhaps 8 to 2. A personal favorite of mine is Winchester Supreme with 1¾ ounces of no. 5 shot in a 3-inch magnum shell. It's a lighter load with higher velocity than most, and has demonstrated superior patterning and killing ability for me on a variety of now-eaten turkeys.

To establish that your turkey gun and loads can perform up to your expectations, one of the most important aspects of preparation is patterning your shotgun. Different loads perform differently in different guns, and it is your job to find out which performs best in your particular gun. You want to see how the shot covers a target at the range in which you might pull the trigger on a hunt.

To do that, set up a clean target that outlines a turkey's head. These are available in many sporting goods stores, or from catalogs. Mount the target on a 4-foot-square sheet of cardboard, which allows you to see your whole pattern. Work your way from 25 to 40 yards, taking shots at different "turkey heads" to ensure that your gun is shooting accurately. Aim at the head/neck area, the most vulnerable part of a heavily feathered turkey's body. Check after each shot to see how many pellets are hitting that vulnerable area.

Though it may only take one well-placed pellet to the head or spinal column to kill a turkey, a good turkey load will put a large number of pellets in the inner core of a pattern. You shouldn't be satisfied if the inner 15-inch-diameter "core" portion of your pattern doesn't show a very high percentage of the pellets at 20 yards. Though the pattern will spread out as the distance is increased, the high percentage of the pellets shot must still remain within the 15-inch core.

Try different loads to establish the best for your gun. If the pattern is going left, right, high or low of the area you are targeting, you can try to adjust for that when shooting. That is a less dependable correction than adding a red-dot sight or a 2X scope that can be adjusted to allow for your gun's performance.

A sling is a great convenience, freeing a hand and allowing for easier walking. The soft Neoprene slings are comfortable on your shoulder. If you can't get camo, get green, brown or black.

BIG GAME RESOURCES

Topographic Maps

You can often obtain topographic maps from backpacking stores and some larger hunting shops. You can also order maps from the U.S. Geological Survey, Distribution Branch, Federal Center, Denver, CO 80225; phone (303)236-5900. First call and ask for a state order map, off of which specific individual maps can be ordered.

DeLorme Mapping Company publishes the popular state-by-state atlas and gazetteer map books. These books have more than a hundred pages of quadrangle maps that cover an entire state. They're great for beginning the planning and research phase of a hunt, as well as for navigating around the state once you get there. Their scale (1:150,000, or about 2½ miles per inch) isn't fine enough to permit using them to pinpoint potential hot spots or identify specific private property boundaries, but they are valuable tools to keep in your office library or your truck.

You can find the atlas and gazetteer map books for your own state in most bookstores and sporting goods stores. Information on ordering volumes not available locally can be obtained from DeLorme Mapping Company, Two DeLorme Drive, P.O. Box 298, Yarmouth, ME 04096; (800)452-5931, or (207)865-4171.

National Forests

These regional headquarters of the U.S. Forest Service can provide a complete list of national forests within their region. From these regional forest headquarters offices, you can obtain current information on logging operations, fires, etc., as well as purchase specific national forest maps. The U.S. Forest Service, and its regional offices nationwide, can also be found on the World Wide Web at www.fs.fed.us.

Region 1 Northern U.S. (Montana, northern Idaho): (406)329-3511

Region 2 Rocky Mountain (Colorado, part of Wyoming): (303)275-5350

Region 3 Southwest (Arizona, New Mexico): (505)842-3076

Region 4 Intermountain (Nevada, southern Idaho, western Wyoming): (801)625-5262

Region 5 Pacific Southwest (California, Nevada): (415)705-2874

Region 6 Pacific Northwest (Oregon, Washington): (503)326-2971

Region 8 Southern U.S.: (404)347-2384

Region 10 Alaska: (610)975-4111

Bureau of Land Management (BLM)

Information on current land status, logging operations, fires, etc., as well as maps of BLM lands are available from the regional offices listed below. The U.S. BLM World Wide Web site (www.blm.gov) provides information and links to regional Web sites.

Alabama: (see Mississippi)
Alaska: (907)271-5960
Arizona: (602)417-9200
Arkansas: (see Mississippi)
California: (916)978-4400
　www.ca.blm.gov
Colorado: (303)239-3600
　www.co.blm.gov
Connecticut: (see Wisconsin)
Delaware: (see Wisconsin)
Florida: (see Mississippi)
Georgia: (see Mississippi)
Idaho: (208)373-3930
　www.id.blm.gov
Illinois: (see Wisconsin)
Indiana: (see Wisconsin)
Iowa: (see Wisconsin)
Kansas: (see New Mexico)
Kentucky: (see Mississippi)
Louisiana: (see Mississippi)
Maine: (see Wisconsin)
Maryland: (see Wisconsin)
Massachusetts: (see Wisconsin)
Michigan: (see Wisconsin)
Minnesota: (see Wisconsin)
Mississippi: (601)977-5400
　www.blm.gov/eso/jdo/index.html
Missouri: (see Wisconsin)
Montana: (406)255-2782
　www.mt.blm.gov
Nebraska: (see Wyoming)
Nevada: (702)861-6400
　www.nv.blm.gov
New Hampshire: (see Wisconsin)
New Jersey: (see Wisconsin)
New Mexico: (505)438-7542
　www.nm.blm.gov

New York: (see Wisconsin)
North Carolina: (see Mississippi)
North Dakota: (see Montana)
Ohio: (see Wisconsin)
Oklahoma: (see New Mexico)
Oregon and Washington:
　(503)952-6027
　www.or.blm.gov
Pennsylvania: (see Wisconsin)
Rhode Island: (see Wisconsin)
South Carolina: (see Mississippi)
South Dakota: (see Montana)
Tennessee: (see Mississippi)
Texas: (see New Mexico)
Utah: (801)539-4001
　www.ut.blm.gov
Vermont: (see Wisconsin)
Virginia: (see Mississippi)
Washington: (see Oregon)
West Virginia: (see Wisconsin)
Wisconsin: (414)297-4400
　www.blm.gov/eso/mdo/index.html
Wyoming: (307)775-6256

Big Game Organizations

Foundation for North American Wild Sheep
720 Allen Ave, Cody, WY 82414
(307)527-6261
www.fnaws.org

Mule Deer Foundation
1005 Terminal Way, Ste 170
Reno, NV 89502
(888)375-DEER, (775)322-6558

National Wild Turkey Federation
PO Box 530, Edgefield, SC 29824
(800)The-NWTF
www.nwtf.org

North American Pronghorn Foundation
1905 CY Avenue, Casper, WY 82604
(307)235-NAPF
www.antelope.org

Rocky Mountain Elk Foundation
PO Box 8249, 2291 W Broadway
Missoula, MT 59807
(800)CALL ELK, (406)523-4500
www.rmef.org

Wildlife Forever
10365 W 70th St
Eden Prairie, MN 55344
(952)833-1522
www.wildlifeforever.org

Record-Keeping Organizations

Boone and Crockett Club
250 Station Drive, Missoula, MT
59801
(406)542-1888
www.boone-crockett.org

Pope & Young Club
P.O. Box 548, Chatfield, MN 55923
(507)867-4144
www.pope-young.org

Safari Club International
4800 West Gates Pass Road
Tucson, AZ 85745
(888)724-HUNT, (602)620-1220
www.safariclub.org

Fish & Game Departments – United States

Alabama Division of Game & Fish
64 N Union St
Montgomery, AL 36130-3020
(334)242-3469
www.dcnr.state.al.us/agfd/

Alaska Department of Fish & Game
PO Box 25526
Juneau, AK 99802-5526
(907)465-4190
www.state.ak.us/adfg

Arizona Game & Fish Department
2221 W Greenway Rd
Phoenix, AZ 85023-4313
(602)942-3000
www.gf.state.az.us

Arkansas Game & Fish Commission
2 Natural Resources Dr
Little Rock, AR 72205-1572
(501)376-0753
www.agfc.com

California Department of Fish &
Game
211 S St
Sacramento, CA 95814
(916)653-7664
www.dfg.ca.gov

Colorado Division of Wildlife
6060 Broadway
Denver, CO 80216-1029
(303)297-1192
www.dnr.state.co.us/wildlife

Connecticut Dept of Environmental
Protection
79 Elm St
Wildlife Division
Hartford, CT 06106
(860)424-3011
www.dep.state.ct.us

Delaware Division of Fish & Wildlife
89 Kings Hwy
PO Box 1401
Dover, DE 19901
(302)739-4431
www.dnrec.state.de.us/fw/fwwel.htm

Florida Game & Freshwater Fish
Commission
620 S Meridian St
Tallahassee, FL 32399-6543
(850)488-4676
www.state.fl.us/fwc

Georgia Wildlife Resources Division
2111 US Hwy 278
Social Circle, GA 30279
(770)918-6416
www.dnr.state.ga.us

Hawaii Division of Forestry & Wildlife
1151 Punchbowl St
Rm 325
Honolulu, HI 96813
(808)587-0166

Idaho Fish & Game Department
PO Box 25
600 S Walnut St
Boise, ID 83712-7729
(208)334-3700
www.state.id.us/fishgame

Illinois Department of Natural
Resources
524 S 2nd St
Springfield, IL 62701-1705
(217)782-6424
www.dnr.state.il.us

Indiana Division of Fish & Wildlife
402 W Washington St
Rm W273
Indianapolis, IN 46204-2739
(317)232-4080
www.dnr.state.in.us/fishwild

Iowa Department of Natural Resources
502 E 9th
Wallace State Office Bldg
Des Moines, IA 50319-0034
(515)281-5918
www.state.ia.us/dnr

Kansas Department of Wildlife &
Parks
512 SE 25th Ave
Pratt, KS 67124-8174
(316)672-5911
www.kdwp.state.ks.us

Kentucky Department of Fish &
Wildlife
1 Game Farm Rd
Frankfurt, KY 40601-3908
(800)858-1549
www.state.ky.us/agencies/fw/kdswr.htm

Louisiana Department of Wildlife &
Fisheries
PO Box 98000
Baton Rouge, LA 70898-9000
(225)765-2800
www.wlf.state.la.us

Maine Department of Inland Fisheries
& Wildlife
41 State House Stn
284 State St
Augusta, ME 04333-0041
(207)287-8000
www.state.me.us/ifw

Maryland Department of Natural
Resources
580 Taylor Ave
Wildlife & Heritage Division
Annapolis, MD 21401-2352
(410)260-8540
www.dnr.state.md.us

Massachusetts Department of
Fisheries & Wildlife
100 Cambridge St
Rm 1902
Boston, MA 02202-0044
(617)626-1590
www.state.ma.us/dfwele

Michigan Department of Natural
Resources
PO Box 30444
Wildlife Division
Lansing, MI 48909-7944
(517)373-1263
www.dnr.state.mi.us/wildlife/

Minnesota Department of Natural
  Resources
500 Lafayette Rd N
Division of Fish & Wildlife
St Paul, MN 55155-4002
(651)296-6157
www.dnr.state.mn.us

Mississippi Dept of Wildlife, Fisheries
  & Parks
PO Box 451
Jackson, MS 39205-0451
(604)362-9212
www.mdwfp.com

Missouri Department of Conservation
2901 W Truman Blvd
PO Box 180
Jefferson City, MO 65109-4999
(573)751-4115
www.conservation.state.mo.us

Montana Dept of Fish, Wildlife &
  Parks
PO Box 200701
1420 E 6th Ave
Helena, MT 59620-0701
(406)444-2535
www.fwp.state.mt.us

Nebraska Game & Parks Commission
2200 N 33rd St
Lincoln, NE 68503-1417
(402)471-0641
www.ngpc.state.ne.us

Nevada Department of Wildlife
PO Box 10678
Reno, NV 89520-0022
(775)688-1500
www.state.nv.us/cnr/nvwildlife/

New Hampshire Fish & Game
  Department
2 Hazen Dr
Concord, NH 03301
(603)271-3211
www.wildlife.state.nh.us

New Jersey Division of Fish, Game &
  Wildlife
PO Box 400
501 E State St 3rd Flr
Trenton, NJ 08609-1101
(609)292-2965
www.state.nj.us/dep/fgw

New Mexico Game & Fish
  Department
PO Box 25112
Santa Fe, NM 87504-5112
(505)827-7911
www.gmfsh.state.nm.us

New York Dept of Environmental
  Conservation
50 Wolf Rd
Rm 151 License Sales Dept
Albany, NY 12233-4790
(518)457-3521
www.dec.state.ny.us

North Carolina Wildlife Resources
  Commission
1722 Mail Service Ctr
Division of Wildlife Mgmt
Raleigh, NC 27699-1722
(919)733-7291
www.state.nc.us/wildlife/

North Dakota State Game & Fish
  Department
100 N Bismarck Expy
Bismarck, ND 58501-5086
(701)328-6300
www.state.nd.us/gnf

Ohio Division of Wildlife
1840 Belcher Dr
Columbus, OH 43224-1329
(614)265-6300
www.dnr.ohio.gov/odnr/wildlife/wildlife.html

Oklahoma Dept of Wildlife
  Conservation
1801 N Lincoln Blvd
Wildlife Division
Oklahoma City, OK 73105-4908
(405)521-2739
www.state.ok.us/~odwc

Oregon Department of Fish & Wildlife
PO Box 59
Portland, OR 97207-0059
(503)872-5268
www.dfw.state.or.us/

Pennsylvania Game Commission
2001 Elmerton Ave
Harrisburg, PA 17110-9797
(717)787-4250
www.pgc.state.pa.us

Rhode Island Division of Fish &
  Wildlife
4808 Tower Hill Rd
Wakefield, RI 02879-2219
(401)277-3075
www.state.ri.us/dem

South Carolina Dept of Natural
  Resources
PO Box 167
Game & Fish Dept
Columbia, SC 29202-0167
(803)734-3888
www.dnr.state.sc.us

South Dakota Game, Fish & Parks
523 E Capitol Ave
Pierre, SD 57501-3182
(605)773-3485
www.state.sd.us/gfp

Tennessee Wildlife Resources Agency
PO Box 40747
Nashville, TN 37204-0747
(615)781-6622
www.state.tn.us/twra.html

Texas Parks & Wildlife Department
4200 Smith School Rd
Austin, TX 78744-3218
(800)792-1112
www.tpwd.state.tx.us

Utah State Dept of Natural Resources
1594 W North Temple
Division of Wildlife Resources
Salt Lake City, UT 84116-3154
(801)538-4700
www.nr.state.ut.us/dwr/!homeypg.htm

Vermont Fish & Wildlife Department
103 S Main St
10 S
Waterbury, VT 05671-0001
(802)241-3700
www.anr.state.vt.us/sw/swhome

Virginia Dept of Game & Inland
  Fisheries
PO Box 11104
Richmond, VA 23230-1104
(804)367-1000
www.dgif.state.va.us

Washington Department of Fish &
  Wildlife
600 Capitol Way N
Olympia, WA 98501-1091
(360)902-2200
www.wa.gov/wdfw/

West Virginia Division of Natural
  Resources
1900 Kanawha Blvd E
Bldg 3 Rm 624
Charleston, WV 25305-1209
(304)558-2758
www.wvweb.com/www/hunting

Wisconsin Dept of Natural Resources
PO Box 7921
Madison, WI 53707-7921
(608)266-2621
www.dnr.state.wi.us

Wyoming Game & Fish Department
5400 Bishop Blvd
Cheyenne, WY 82006-0001
(307)777-4600
www.gf.state.wy.us

Fish & Game Departments – Canada

Alberta Fisheries & Wildlife
Management Division
Main Flr South Tower Petroleum Plaza
9915 108th St
Edmonton, AB T5K 2G8
(780)427-5185
www.env.gov.ab.ca/

BC Ministry of the Environment,
  Lands & Parks
PO Box 9359 Wildlife Branch
Stn Provincial Gov
Victoria, BC V8W 9M2
(250)387-3205
www.env.gov.bc.ca

Manitoba Dept of Natural Resources
200 Salteaux Cresc
Winnipeg, MB R3J 3W3
(800)214-6495
www.gov.mb.ca/natres

New Brunswick Dept of Natural
  Resources
Fish & Wildlife Branch
PO Box 6000
Fredricton, NB E3B 5H1
(506)453-2440
www.nbgov.nb.ca

Newfoundland Dept of Forest
  Resources & Agrifoods
Wildlife Division, Bldg 810
Pleasantville
PO Box 8700
St John's, NF A1B 4J6
(709)729-2630
www.public.gov.nf.ca.tourism

Northwest Territories Resources,
  Wildlife & Economic Development
PO Box 28
Tuktoyaktuk, NT X0E 1C0
(867)977-2350

Nova Scotia Dept of Natural Resources
PO Box 698
Halifax, NS B3J 2T9
(902)424-5935
www.natr.gov.ns.ca

Ontario Natural Resources Info Center
PO Box 7000
300 Water St 1st Flr
Peterborough, ON K9J 8M5
(705)755-2000
www.mnr.gov.on.ca

Prince Edward Island Dept of
  Technology & Environment
Fish & Wildlife Division
PO Box 2000 11 Kent St
Charlettetown, PE C1A 7N8
(902)368-4683
www.gov.pe.ca/

Quebec Dept of Recreation
Fish & Wildlife Division
150 Rene Levesque E 8th Flr
Quebec City, PQ G1R 4Y1
(418)643-6662

Saskatchewan Environment Resource
  Management
Fish & Wildlife Branch Rm 436
3211 Albert St
Regina, SK S4S 5W6
(306)787-2314
www.gov.sk.ca/govt/environ/

Yukon Renewable Resources
Fish & Wildlife Branch
PO Box 2703
Whitehorse, YK Y1A 2C6
(867)667-5221
www.gov.yk.ca/

INDEX